Chapter 1: "Understanding Inflation"

The Silent Thief

The Seminar Begins:

The air was thick with curiosity and concern. Amit scanned the crowded seminar room, noticing the diverse group around him—young professionals with hopeful eyes, middle-aged couples scribbling notes, and retirees clutching their financial statements. Each one carried the same silent question: "Am I losing money without realizing it?"

Arjun Mehta, a tall, confident financial advisor, stepped onto the stage. The murmurs subsided.

"Good evening," he began. "Today, we're discussing something that silently erodes your wealth: Inflation."

He held up a ☐ 100 note.

"What can this buy you today?"

The audience responded:

- "Two cups of coffee!"
- "A small pizza!"
- "Maybe a movie ticket?"

Arjun's smile faded. "Thirty years ago, this same ☐ 100 bought an entire grocery cart. Today, it barely covers a few items. That's inflation."

The Story of ₹100: A Journey through Time

Amit's pen danced across his notebook. Inflation: The rate at which the price of goods and services rises, eroding purchasing power.

Arjun continued, "Imagine saving ₹10 lakh today, thinking it secures your future. At 6% inflation, in 10 years, it will only have the buying power of about ₹5.6 lakh."

He wrote on the whiteboard:

Future Value Formula:
Real Value = Current Savings / (1 + Inflation Rate)^n

Example:
If inflation averages 6%, and you have ₹10 lakh today, in 5 years:
Real Value = ₹10,00,000 / (1.06)^5 ≈ ₹7,47,000

Amit's eyes widened. "So, saving alone isn't enough?"

Flashback: Amit's Father's Lesson

Amit's thoughts drifted back to 1995. He was at the market with his father. A ₹100 note bought a bag full of vegetables.

His father had said, "Next year, this ₹100 won't be enough. Prices go up. That's why we plan ahead."

Back then, the warning seemed abstract. Now, it felt prophetic.

Types of Inflation: Breaking it Down

Am I losing Money Without realizing it?

This book has the potential to be a game-changer for readers aiming for financial stability. Here's how it can help:

1. Building Financial Awareness

By breaking down complex financial concepts into easily understandable ideas, the book will make readers more aware of the importance of savings, investments, and inflation. Understanding how inflation affects purchasing power and savings will motivate them to think strategically about how they manage money.

2. Creating a Long-Term Financial Strategy

The book emphasizes the importance of planning and provides actionable strategies for long-term wealth-building. It teaches readers not only how to save but also how to invest wisely and diversify their portfolios to protect against inflation. This ensures that their wealth grows over time rather than stagnating.

3. Encouraging Smart Investments

With real-life examples and financial tools like stocks, bonds, ETFs, and inflation-protected securities, the book gives readers the knowledge they need to make smart investments. This helps them move beyond traditional savings methods and take calculated risks that have the potential for higher returns.

4. Risk Management and Emotional Discipline

One of the most valuable aspects of the book is its focus on emotional discipline and risk management. By teaching readers how to remain calm in times of market volatility and stick to their financial strategies, it empowers them to make rational decisions that support their long-term goals.

5. Empowering Financial Independence

With the advice on building emergency funds, managing debt, automating savings, and understanding tax strategies, readers will be able to create a more secure financial foundation. Over time, this leads to greater financial independence, reducing stress and increasing confidence in their ability to handle financial challenges.

6. Practical Financial Tools

By introducing readers to tools and resources like budgeting apps, risk assessments, and portfolio tracking, the book helps them implement financial strategies efficiently. These tools can simplify financial management and increase the chances of achieving financial stability.

In summary, the book provides not only the knowledge but also the practical steps and mindset needed to help readers become financially stable and resilient in an ever-changing economic environment. By following the insights and strategies shared, readers can protect and grow their wealth, which is essential for long-term financial security.

Arjun wrote three types of inflation on the board:

1. **Demand-Pull Inflation:**
   Cause: Demand exceeds supply.
   Example: During festivals, the price of sweets soars because everyone is buying them.
2. **Cost-Push Inflation:**
   Cause: Higher production costs (wages, raw materials) raise prices.
   Example: Rising fuel prices increase transportation costs, making goods more expensive.
3. **Built-In Inflation:**
   Cause: Wages increase to keep up with living costs, raising prices.
   Example: Salary hikes lead to higher spending power, but goods become pricier.

Amit's Personal Battle with Inflation:

In 2010, Amit earned ☐ 20,000 a month. Rent was ☐ 5,000, groceries ☐ 3,000. Life felt secure.
Today, his income had tripled to ☐ 60,000, but rent was ☐ 20,000, groceries ☐ 10,000.

"Why do I feel like I'm running but getting nowhere?" he wondered.

Arjun's voice cut through his thoughts. "You're on a treadmill called inflation. If your income doesn't outpace it, you stay in the same place."

The Silent Thief Analogy:

Arjun leaned closer to the mic. "Inflation is like a slow leak in a tire. At first, you don't notice it. But over time, it can stop your journey. Your savings are that tire. Without proper investment, your wealth deflates."

Interactive Moment: Inflation Calculator

Arjun handed out worksheets. "Calculate how much your savings will be worth in 10 years with 5% inflation."

Amit's heart sank. His ☐ 10 lakh would shrink to ☐ 6.3 lakh.

He turned to Priya, whispering, "We need a new plan."

Historical Perspective: Inflation's Global Impact

Arjun shared historical examples:

- **Germany, 1920s:** Hyperinflation made money worthless. People carried wheelbarrows of cash to buy bread.
- **Venezuela, 2018:** Annual inflation reached 1,000,000%. Essentials became unaffordable.

"This isn't just history," Arjun warned. "Unchecked inflation can devastate any economy."

The Emotional Toll of Inflation:

Amit recalled a recent grocery trip with Priya:

- **2015 Bill:** ☐ 5,000
- **Today's Bill:** ☐ 8,500 for the same items.

"We're spending more but buying the same things," he lamented.

Priya nodded. "Saving isn't enough. We need to invest wisely."

End-of-Chapter Takeaway: Key Insights

1. Inflation is inevitable: You can't stop it, but you can outpace it.
2. Savings lose value: Without growth, you're losing money daily.

Reflection for Readers:

"If inflation continues at 6%, will your current savings secure your future goals? Are you ready to learn how to fight back?"

Next Chapter Preview:

Chapter 2: The Impact on Savings — Dreams Deferred
Amit and Priya face a harsh realization: their dream of sending Meera to college might be slipping away. How can they adapt their savings strategy to outpace inflation and secure their future?

Chapter 2: The Impact on Savings — Dreams Deferred

Amit and Priya face a harsh realization: their dream of sending Meera to college might be slipping away. How can they adapt their savings strategy to outpace inflation and secure their future?

The Family Discussion:

Amit sat on the balcony, staring at the distant city lights. Priya joined him, a cup of chai in her hands. The evening air was heavy with their silent worries.

Priya: "We've been saving for Meera's college fund since she was born. But after today's seminar, I'm scared. What if we're still short?"

Amit nodded.

Amit: "I've done the math. If college fees grow at 8% per year, our savings won't be enough."

Priya: "Then what's the point of saving?"

Understanding Real Returns:

The next day, Amit visited Arjun's office.

Arjun smiled as he pulled out a whiteboard.

"Let's talk about real returns."

Definition:
Real return = Nominal return (from your savings or investment) - Inflation rate.

Example:
Fixed Deposit: Offers 6% interest.
Inflation Rate: 6%.

Arjun: "What's your real return?"

Amit: "Zero?"

Arjun: "Exactly. Even though your money grows on paper, its purchasing power remains the same. It's like running in place."

Amit's Father's Lesson:

Amit remembered a conversation with his father 15 years ago:

Father: "In 1980, I saved ☐ 50,000 in an account. It's ☐ 5 lakh now. But a car that cost ☐ 50,000 then costs ☐ 8 lakh today. I saved, but I didn't grow."

Amit: "So, investing is the only way?"

Father: "Yes. But smart investing."

Comparing Savings vs. Investment:

Arjun laid out two scenarios:

1. **Traditional Savings Account:**
   - ☐ 1 lakh saved
   - Interest Rate: 4%
   - Inflation: 6%

   After 10 years:

   - ☐ 1 lakh becomes ☐ 1.48 lakh.
   - **Purchasing Power:** ☐ 88,000 in today's terms.
2. **Investment in Equity Funds:**
   - Average Return: 10%

   After 10 years:

   - ☐ 1 lakh becomes ☐ 2.59 lakh.
   - **Real Growth:** ☐ 1.95 lakh in today's terms.

Arjun: "Savings accounts are safe but don't protect you from inflation. Investments carry risk but grow your wealth."

A Wake-Up Call:

Amit and Priya visited their bank manager, Mr. Sharma.

Mr. Sharma: "Your FD is safe. You won't lose money."

Amit: "But won't inflation eat into it?"

Mr. Sharma hesitated. "Well… yes, but it's low-risk."

Amit: "Low risk, low reward. We need to rethink our strategy."

Takeaway Insights:

1. **Safety vs. Growth:** Savings accounts and FDs are low-risk but offer minimal protection against inflation.
2. **Investing in Assets:** Consider equity, mutual funds, and gold for better long-term returns.

Reflection Question:

"Are your savings growing fast enough to keep up with your dreams?"

Next Chapter Preview:

Chapter 3: Smart Investments — Turning the Tide
Amit and Priya explore investment options. Which ones will help them beat inflation without risking it all?

Chapter 3: "Smart Investments"
Turning the Tide

Rohan's Portfolio Breakdown:

In Rohan's living room, Amit and Priya sat, curious to learn more.
Rohan: "Let me show you my actual portfolio. Real examples make it easier."

Investment Overview:

- **Equity Mutual Funds:** 50%
- **Debt Funds:** 20%
- **Gold ETFs:** 10%
- **Real Estate:** 15%
- **Emergency Fund:** 5%

Why Focus on Equities?

Priya: "Why so much in equities?"
Rohan: "Long-term growth. Let's compare."

Example: Equity Mutual Funds vs. Fixed Deposits

Scenario: Invest ☐ 10,000/month for 15 years.

1. **Fixed Deposit (6% Interest):**
    - **Total Investment:** ☐ 18 lakh
    - **Maturity Value:** ☐ 29.5 lakh
2. **Equity Mutual Fund (12% Return):**
    - **Total Investment:** ☐ 18 lakh
    - **Maturity Value:** ☐ 50.7 lakh

Rohan: "See the difference? Equities can double your returns!"
Priya: "But aren't they risky?"
Rohan: "Yes, but SIPs spread out the risk."

Tools for Choosing Mutual Funds:

Rohan's Tips:

- **Screener Tools:** Compare funds on apps like ET Money, Groww, and Zerodha Coin.
- **Risk Assessment Calculators:** Check your risk tolerance using Moneycontrol or Morningstar.

Rohan: "Never invest blindly. Always research using these tools."

Understanding Asset Allocation:

Amit: "How do we decide the right mix?"

Rohan's Rule: Your age guides your strategy.

- **20s-30s:** High risk, high reward (70% Equity, 20% Debt, 10% Gold)
- **40s-50s:** Moderate risk (50% Equity, 30% Debt, 20% Gold/Real Estate)
- **60s+:** Low risk (20% Equity, 50% Debt, 30% Gold)

Example:
"Rohan's cousin invested heavily in stocks at 25 but shifted to debt funds at 40."
Priya: "So, our strategy changes with age?"
Rohan: "Exactly! Review it annually."

The Power of Gold ETFs:

Priya: "Why not just buy jewelry?"
Rohan: "Gold ETFs are better: digital, easy to store, and track gold prices."

Example:

- **Gold Price in 2010:** ☐ 18,000/10 gm
- **Gold Price in 2023:** ☐ 60,000/10 gm

Rohan: "Gold isn't just tradition—it's an inflation shield."

Debt Funds: The Safety Layer:

Rohan explained:

- **Liquid Funds:** Better than savings accounts for extra cash.
- **Corporate Bonds:** Higher returns than FDs (8% vs. 6%) but slightly riskier.

Priya: "So, debt funds balance the risk?"
Rohan: "Exactly! They cushion equity volatility."

Practical Tools Mentioned:

- **Investment Apps:** Groww, Zerodha, ET Money
- **Portfolio Trackers:** Moneycontrol, INDmoney
- **Risk Calculators:** Available on most financial sites

Key Takeaways:

1. **Start Small:** Even ₹500/month grows over time.
2. **Diversify:** Balance risk and reward across different assets.
3. **Research:** Use tools; don't follow trends blindly.

Reflection Question:

"Are you managing your portfolio like a business—diversifying and reviewing regularly?"

Next Chapter Preview:

Chapter 4: Compounding — The Eighth Wonder of the World
Amit and Priya learn how small, consistent investments can snowball into significant wealth. Will they leverage this "wonder" for their future?

Chapter 4: "Compounding"

The Eighth Wonder of the World

The Magic of Compounding:

Amit and Priya returned to Rohan's home, intrigued by his mention of "the magic of compounding."

Rohan: "Albert Einstein called compounding the eighth wonder of the world. Let me show you why."

Simple vs. Compound Interest:

Example Scenario:

- **Principal:** ☐ 1 lakh
- **Interest Rate:** 10% per year
- **Duration:** 10 years

1. Simple Interest:

- **Formula:** Principal × Rate × Time
- **Result:** ☐ 1 lakh × 10% × 10 years = ☐ 2 lakh

2. Compound Interest:

- **Formula:** $A = P(1 + r/n)^{(nt)}$
- **Result:** ☐ 2.59 lakh

Amit: "Why does compound interest give more?"
Rohan: "With compounding, you earn interest on both your principal

and the interest you've earned. Your money works harder over time."

Real-Life Example — Two Friends:

Case Study: Rahul and Ravi

- **Rahul:** Starts investing ☐ 5,000/month at 25, stops at 35 (10 years)
- **Ravi:** Starts investing ☐ 5,000/month at 35, continues until 55 (20 years)

Assuming 12% annual returns:

- **Rahul's Total Investment:** ☐ 6 lakh → Grows to ☐ **1.7 crore** by 55
- **Ravi's Total Investment:** ☐ 12 lakh → Grows to ☐ **1.2 crore** by 55

Priya: "Rahul invested for a shorter time but earned more!"
Rohan: "That's the power of starting early. **Time in the market matters more than timing the market.**"

Tools to Plan Your Growth:

Rohan's Recommendations:

- **Compound Interest Calculators:** Available on **Groww, ET Money, and Moneycontrol.**
- **Excel Formula:**
    - **Compound Interest:** `=FV(rate, nper, pmt, pv, type)`

- **Example:** `=FV(0.10/12, 240, -5000, 0)` for ₹5,000/month over 20 years.

Priya's 10-Year Challenge:

Rohan's Experiment:
"Priya, invest just ₹1,000/month for 10 years."

- **Initial Amount:** ₹0
- **Monthly Investment:** ₹1,000
- **Interest Rate:** 12%

Result: Future Value after 10 years = ₹**2.32 lakh**

Priya: "₹1,000 a month turns into ₹2.32 lakh?"
Rohan: "Yes! **Start small, but stay consistent.**"

The Snowball Effect:

Rohan's Analogy:
"Imagine rolling a small snowball down a hill. It gathers more snow, growing bigger as it rolls."

- **Early Investments:** Like starting the snowball.
- **Reinvesting Returns:** Adds more layers, growing your wealth exponentially.

Key Takeaways:

1. **Start Early:** Time is your biggest asset.
2. **Stay Consistent:** Regular, small investments grow over time.

3. **Reinvest Returns:** Let your money work for you.

Reflection Question:

"Are you leveraging the power of compounding in your financial journey?"

Next Chapter Preview:

Chapter 5: Inflation-Proof Strategies — Protecting Your Future
Amit and Priya discover how to shield their savings from inflation, ensuring long-term financial security.

Chapter 5: "Inflation-Proof Strategies" Protecting Your Future

The Silent Killer — Inflation's Impact:

Amit, Priya, and Rohan gathered around the kitchen table, sipping chai. Rohan pulled out an old grocery bill.

Rohan: "Look at this bill from 2010:

- **Milk:** ☐ 20/litre → ☐ **65/litre** today
- **Rice:** ☐ 30/kg → ☐ **80/kg**
- **Petrol:** ☐ 50/litre → ☐ **110/litre**

Amit: "Everything costs double or triple now!"
Rohan: "That's inflation. The same ☐ 100 buys less over time."

Understanding Inflation:

Priya: "What exactly is inflation?"
Rohan: "Inflation is the rate at which prices of goods and services rise."

Example:

- **Current Inflation Rate:** ~6% in India
- ☐ **1 lakh today:** In 10 years, it's worth only ☐ **53,000** in today's terms.

Investment Options to Beat Inflation:

Rohan's List of Investments:

1. **Equities (Stocks):** Average return **12-15%**
2. **Real Estate:** Returns **8-10%** per year
3. **Gold:** Long-term returns around **8%**
4. **Index Funds (e.g., Nifty 50):** Track the market's performance

Example — Nifty 50 Growth:

- **2014:** ~7,000 points → **2024:** ~22,000 points

Rohan: "These investments help protect your savings from losing value."

Real Estate — A Strong Shield:

Amit: "What about real estate?"
Rohan: "It's a great hedge against inflation, especially in growing cities."

Case Study:

- **Property in Patna (2010):** ☐ 20 lakh
- **Value in 2024:** ☐ 80 lakh

Rohan: "Remember, real estate needs careful planning. Consider maintenance costs and how quickly you can sell."

Safe Options — TIPS & Bonds:

Priya: "Are there safer options?"
Rohan: "Yes! Government bonds protect against inflation."

Examples:

- **Sovereign Gold Bonds (SGBs):** 2.5% interest + gold price increase
- **Inflation-Indexed Bonds (IIBs):** Adjust with inflation

Diversifying Your Investments:

Rohan's Advice: "Don't rely on just one type of investment. Diversify."

Sample Inflation-Proof Portfolio:

- **Equity:** 50%
- **Gold/Real Estate:** 20%
- **Debt Instruments (like bonds):** 20%
- **Cash/Emergency Fund:** 10%

Tools:

- Use apps like **ET Money** to manage and track your portfolio.

Practical Tips — Fighting Inflation Daily:

Priya: "How do we manage daily expenses?"
Rohan's Tips:

1. **Bulk Buying:** Purchase non-perishable items at wholesale rates.
2. **Invest in Skills:** Learn new skills to increase your income.

3. **Use Budget Apps:** Track spending with apps like **Walnut** or **Money View**.

Key Takeaways:

1. **Understand Inflation:** Know how it reduces your money's value.
2. **Invest Wisely:** Choose investments that beat inflation.
3. **Diversify:** Spread your risk across different assets.
4. **Stay Informed:** Monitor inflation trends and adjust your plan.

Reflection Question:

"Are your current investments outpacing inflation? If not, how can you adjust?"

Next Chapter Preview:

Chapter 6: Emergency Funds — Preparing for the Unexpected
A sudden crisis tests Amit and Priya's financial readiness. Rohan shows them how to build a strong emergency fund.

Chapter 6: "Emergency Funds"
Preparing for the Unexpected

The Unexpected Call:

Late at night, Amit's phone buzzed. It was his brother.

Amit: "What happened?"
Brother: "Papa had an accident. He's stable but needs surgery."

The next morning, they rushed to the hospital.

Priya: "How much will the surgery cost?"
Doctor: "₹ 3 lakhs."
Amit: "I only have ₹ 50,000 in savings… What do we do now?"

Why Emergency Funds Are Essential:

Rohan met them at the hospital.

Rohan: "This is why everyone needs an emergency fund. It's a financial cushion for unexpected events like this."

How Much Should You Save?

Priya: "How much should we have in an emergency fund?"

Rohan explained:

- **Target:** Save 3-6 months' worth of expenses.
- **Example:** If your monthly expenses are ₹ 30,000, aim for **₹ 90,000 to ₹ 1.8 lakh.**
- **Tip:** Keep this money in a separate, easily accessible account.

Where to Keep Emergency Funds:

Rohan: "It's important where you save the money."

Options:

1. **High-Interest Savings Account:**
   - Quick access but lower returns.
2. **Liquid Mutual Funds:**
   - Returns: **4-6% per year.**
   - Easily withdrawable when needed.
3. **Fixed Deposits (FDs):**
   - Higher returns but a penalty for early withdrawal.

Example:

- ₹ 1 lakh in a liquid fund at 5%:
  After 1 year: ₹ **1.05 lakh.**

Real-Life Example — Job Loss:

Rohan's Story:

- **Manish**, an IT professional, lost his job during the 2020 pandemic.
- **Had a 6-month emergency fund:** ₹ 3 lakh saved.
- **Manish:** "It kept my family afloat until I found a new job."

How to Build Your Emergency Fund:

Priya: "Where do we start?"

Rohan's Steps:

1. **Set a Target:** Calculate 3-6 months of expenses.
2. **Start Small:** Save ☐ 1,000 or ☐ 2,000 each month.
3. **Automate Savings:** Set up auto-debits from your salary.
4. **Cut Unnecessary Expenses:** Redirect that money to your fund.

Tools You Can Use:

- **Budget Apps:** Track spending (Apps like **YNAB** or **Mint**).
- **Recurring Deposits (RD):** Save a fixed amount monthly.

Mistakes to Avoid:

Rohan's Warnings:

1. **Avoid Using Credit Cards for Emergencies:**
    - High-interest debt can trap you.
2. **Don't Invest Emergency Funds in Stocks:**
    - Stocks are volatile and risky for emergencies.
3. **Refill the Fund:**
    - If you use it, prioritize rebuilding it.

Example:
Amit: "I once used my emergency fund for a vacation."
Rohan: "It's for emergencies only, not luxury spending."

Amit and Priya's Plan:

Priya: "We need to start now."

Their Plan:

- **Monthly Savings Target:** ₹ 5,000
- **Goal:** ₹ 1.8 lakh in 3 years.

Method:

- ₹ 2,500 in a savings account
- ₹ 2,500 in a liquid fund

Key Takeaways:

1. **Build a Buffer:** Emergency funds come before aggressive investments.
2. **Keep It Accessible:** Quick access is key during crises.
3. **Be Disciplined:** Use it strictly for emergencies.

Reflection Question:

"If a financial emergency happened tomorrow, could you handle it without borrowing money?"

Next Chapter Preview:

Chapter 7: Insurance — Your Financial Safety Net
A sudden health scare teaches Amit and Priya the importance of insurance. Rohan explains how insurance protects their financial future.

Chapter 7: "Insurance"

Your Financial Safety Net

A Close Call:

A few months later, Priya fell ill and was hospitalized.

Amit: "The doctor said she needs surgery. It will cost ☐ 5 lakh."
Rohan: "Do you have health insurance?"
Amit: "No... I didn't think we'd ever need it."
Rohan: "That's a common mistake. Insurance isn't just an expense — it's financial protection."

What is Insurance?

Rohan explained:
Insurance is a contract where you pay a regular amount (called a **premium**), and the insurer covers specific financial risks, like health, life, or property.

Types of Insurance:

1. **Health Insurance:**
    - **Covers:** Medical expenses.
    - **Why important?** Medical costs are rising by **10-15% each year**. One illness can wipe out your savings.

   Example:

- **Bypass surgery cost:**
    - 2005: ☐ 1 lakh
    - 2024: ☐ 4-5 lakh
2. **Life Insurance:**
    - **Covers:** Provides financial support to your family if you pass away.
    - **Amit:** "Who depends on your income?"
    - **Amit:** "Priya and our daughter."
    - **Rohan:** "Life insurance ensures they are financially secure if something happens to you."
3. **Motor Insurance:**
    - **Covers:** Vehicle-related damages, accidents, and third-party liabilities.
    - **Mandatory by law.**
4. **Home Insurance:**
    - **Covers:** Damages from fire, theft, or natural disasters.

Health Insurance: A Must-Have

Priya: "Is health insurance really worth it?"
Rohan: "Yes. Medical expenses are rising. Without insurance, you might lose your savings."

Types of Health Plans:

- **Individual Plan:** For one person.
- **Family Floater Plan:** Covers the whole family under one policy.
- **Critical Illness Cover:** For serious diseases like cancer or heart attack.

Example:

- **Neha's Policy:** ☐ 10 lakh coverage for ☐ 15,000/year.
- **Hospital Bill:** ☐ 3 lakh (dengue).

- **Neha paid only ☐ 10,000; insurance covered the rest.**

Life Insurance: Protect Your Family

Types of Life Insurance:

1. **Term Insurance:**
    - **Pure protection:** No savings or maturity benefits.
    - **High coverage, low premium.**
    - **Example:** ☐ 1 crore cover for ☐ 10,000/year.
2. **Endowment Plans:**
    - Combines insurance with savings.
3. **ULIPs (Unit Linked Insurance Plans):**
    - Combines insurance with investments.

Why Term Insurance?

- **Affordable:** High coverage at a low cost.
- **Essential:** Especially for breadwinners.

Motor and Home Insurance:

Motor Insurance:

- **Mandatory:** Protects against accidents and theft.
- **Example:** Repair cost ☐ 1 lakh; insurance covered ☐ 80,000.

Home Insurance:

- **Protects:** Against fire, theft, and natural disasters.
- **Example:** House damaged in a flood; insurance paid for repairs.

Choosing the Right Policy:

Rohan's Tips:

1. **Assess Your Needs:** Health, life, motor, and home.
2. **Compare Policies:** Use online tools like **Policybazaar** or **Coverfox**.
3. **Read the Fine Print:** Check exclusions, waiting periods, and claim processes.

Helpful Tools:

- **IRDAI Website:** To find verified insurers.
- **Claim Settlement Ratio:** Shows how reliable an insurer is.

Amit and Priya's Plan:

Amit: "We need to get insured immediately."

Steps They Took:

1. **Health Insurance:** ☐ 10 lakh family floater plan.
2. **Term Life Insurance:** ☐ 1 crore cover for Amit.
3. **Motor Insurance:** Renewed with comprehensive coverage.

Priya: "I feel more secure knowing we're protected."

Key Takeaways:

1. **Insurance is Essential:** Protects you from financial shocks.
2. **Start with Health and Life Insurance:** Prioritize your family's needs.

3. **Compare Policies Wisely:** Use tools to choose the best coverage.

Reflection Question:

"Are you protected against life's unexpected events? If not, which insurance do you need first?"

Next Chapter Preview:

Chapter 8: Investing in the Right Instruments — Growing Wealth Smartly
Rohan guides Amit and Priya through choosing the best investments to beat inflation and grow their wealth.

Chapter 8: "Investing in the Right Instruments"

Growing Wealth Smartly

Why Invest?

Amit and Priya met Rohan at a café, curious about the next step after securing insurance.
Amit: "We've set up insurance and an emergency fund. Now what?"
Rohan: "Investing. It's how you grow your money and beat inflation."

Priya: "But isn't investing risky?"
Rohan: "Yes, but not investing is riskier. Inflation erodes your savings over time."

Understanding Inflation

Inflation: Prices of goods and services increase over time.
Example:

- **Inflation Rate:** 6% per year.
- **Savings Account Interest:** 3% per year.

Rohan: "If you keep ▢ 1 lakh in a savings account, it becomes ▢ 1.03 lakh in a year. But to buy the same things next year, you'll need ▢ 1.06 lakh due to inflation. So, you're losing money."

Investment Options Simplified

Rohan introduced key investment types:

1. **Stocks (Equity):**
   - **High risk, high return.**
   - **Example:** Ramesh invested ₹50,000 in TCS shares in 2010. Now worth ₹4 lakh.
   - **Tool:** Use apps like **Zerodha** for trading.
2. **Mutual Funds:**
   - **Professionally managed.**
   - **Types:** Equity, Debt, Hybrid.
   - **SIP (Systematic Investment Plan):**
     - **Example:** Investing ₹5,000/month in a Nifty 50 Fund.
     - **Result:** Could grow to ₹12-15 lakh in 10 years (assuming 12% annual returns).
   - **Tools: Groww, ET Money, Coin by Zerodha.**
3. **Debt Instruments:**
   - **Low risk, stable returns.**
   - **Examples:** FDs, PPF, Bonds.
   - **PPF Example:**
     - Invest ₹1.5 lakh/year for 15 years.
     - Grows to ₹40 lakh at 7.1% interest.
4. **Gold:**
   - **Hedge against inflation.**
   - **Types:** Physical, digital, ETFs.
   - **Example:** ₹1 lakh invested in gold in 2005 is now worth ₹6 lakh.
5. **Real Estate:**
   - **Long-term investment.**
   - **Example:** A flat bought for ₹20 lakh in 2010 is now worth ₹70 lakh.

Choosing the Right Mix: Asset Allocation

Rohan: "Your investment mix depends on your goals and risk tolerance."

Priya: "How do we decide?"

Rohan's Tips:

1. **Short-Term Goals (1-3 years):**
   - Use Debt Funds, FDs.
   - Example: Saving for a car.
2. **Medium-Term Goals (3-7 years):**
   - Choose Balanced or Hybrid Funds.
   - Example: Child's education.
3. **Long-Term Goals (7+ years):**
   - Focus on Equity Funds, Stocks, Real Estate.
   - Example: Retirement planning.

Practical Plan for Amit and Priya

Goal: Buy a house in 10 years.

- **Target Amount:** ₹50lakh.
- **Plan:** Start a monthly SIP of ₹10,000 in an equity mutual fund.
- **Expected Returns:** 12% annually.

Tool: Use **ET Money Goal Planner** to calculate SIPs.

Avoid Common Investment Mistakes

Rohan shared lessons from real-life mistakes:

1. **Chasing Quick Returns:**
    - Rahul lost ₹5lakh on a stock tip scam.
2. **Not Diversifying:**
    - Putting all money in one stock is risky.
3. **Stopping SIPs During Market Crashes:**
    - Meera stopped investing during a downturn and missed the rebound.

Key Takeaways:

1. **Investing Beats Inflation:** Your money grows over time.
2. **Diversify:** Spread investments across different assets.
3. **Stay Consistent:** Avoid making emotional decisions during market changes.

Reflection Question:

"What's your financial goal, and how can you start investing towards it today?"

Next Chapter Preview:

Chapter 9: Tax Planning — Saving Smartly
Rohan teaches Amit and Priya how to legally reduce their taxes using smart investments like ELSS and PPF.

Chapter 9: "Tax Planning"
Saving Smartly

Why Tax Planning Matters

Amit and Priya are stressed about taxes. Rohan visits them to explain how they can save money legally by using tax-saving tools.

Priya: "We pay so much tax every year. Can't we reduce it?"
Rohan: "Definitely! By using deductions and exemptions, you can lower your taxable income and keep more money in your pocket."

Understanding the Basics

1. Income Tax Slabs:

- ₹0- ₹3lakh: No tax
- ₹3lakh - ₹6lakh: 5% tax
- ₹6lakh - ₹9lakh: 10% tax
- ₹9lakh - ₹12lakh: 15% tax
- ₹12lakh - ₹15lakh: 20% tax
- **Above** ₹15lakh: 30% tax

2. Exemptions vs. Deductions:

- **Exemptions:** Reduce taxable income (like HRA for rent or a standard deduction).
- **Deductions:** Investments or expenses you can claim under different sections (like 80C or 80D).

Top Tax-Saving Instruments

Section 80C: Save up to ₹1.5 Lakh

1. **Equity Linked Savings Scheme (ELSS):**
   - **Lock-in:** 3 years
   - **Returns:** 12-15% (historically)
   - **Example:** If Priya invests ₹1.5lakh, she can save ₹46,800 in tax (if she's in the 30% tax bracket).
2. **Public Provident Fund (PPF):**
   - **Lock-in:** 15 years
   - **Interest Rate:** 7.1%
   - **Example:** Amit invests ₹1.5lakh/year. After 15 years, it grows to about ₹40lakh.
3. **National Pension System (NPS):**
   - **Extra Deduction:** ₹50,000 (Section 80CCD(1B))
   - **Returns:** 8-10%
   - **Example:** Investing ₹50,000 saves ₹15,000 in tax (for a 30% bracket taxpayer).
4. **Life Insurance Premiums:**
   - Only applicable if the premium is ≤ 10% of the sum assured.
   - **Example:** Priya pays ₹30,000 annually for a ₹5lakh policy. The entire premium is tax-deductible.

Health Insurance and Section 80D

- **Deduction for Health Insurance:**
  - **Self, spouse, and children:** Up to ₹25,000
  - **Parents (senior citizens):** Up to ₹50,000

Example:
Amit spends:

- ₹20,000 for family insurance
- ₹40,000 for his parents' insurance
- **Total Deduction:** ₹60,000

Home Loan Benefits

Amit: "We're buying a house soon. Will it help with taxes?"
Rohan: "Yes! You get benefits on both the principal and interest."

1. **Principal Repayment:**
    - Deduct up to ₹1.5lakh (under Section 80C).
2. **Interest Repayment:**
    - Deduct up to ₹2lakh/year (under Section 24(b)).

Example:

- **Loan Amount:** ₹30lakh
- **Annual Interest:** ₹2.5lakh
- **Deduction:** ₹2lakh

Real-Life Tax Plan Example

Case: Ramesh, a software engineer earning ₹ 15 lakh/year.

- **80C:** ₹1.5lakh (ELSS + PPF)
- **80D:** ₹50,000 (Health Insurance)
- **NPS:** ₹50,000
- **Home Loan Interest:** ₹2lakh

Total Tax Savings: ₹ 3.5 lakh!

Tools for Easy Tax Planning

- **Tax Calculators:** ClearTax, Income Tax India portal
- **Investment Platforms:** Groww, Zerodha, ET Money

Key Takeaways:

1. **Plan Early:** Don't wait until the last minute.
2. **Use the Right Mix:** Balance equity, debt, and insurance.
3. **Save More, Stress Less:** Proper planning means more money for your goals.

Reflection Question:

"How much tax could you save with better planning this year?"

Next Chapter:
Creating a Financial Plan — Roadmap to Wealth
Amit and Priya will learn to build a personalized plan, combining everything they've learned.

Chapter 10: "Creating a Financial Plan"

Roadmap to Wealth

A Clear Path to Your Dreams

Amit and Priya meet with Rohan to understand how to organize their savings and investments.

Priya: "We've learned about saving, investing, and tax planning. How do we combine all this?"
Rohan: "That's where financial planning comes in. Think of it as creating a roadmap for your financial journey."

Step 1: Define Your Goals

Rohan: "Start by identifying your goals: short-term, medium-term, and long-term."

- **Short-Term (1-3 years):**
  Examples: Vacation, buying a car, emergency fund.
- **Medium-Term (3-7 years):**
  Examples: Down payment for a house, child's education.
- **Long-Term (7+ years):**
  Examples: Retirement, child's marriage.

Priya: "Our goals are to buy a house, save for our daughter's education, and retire comfortably."
Rohan: "Let's plan for each goal separately."

Step 2: Build an Emergency Fund

Rohan: "Your emergency fund is your financial safety net."

- **How much to save:** 3-6 months of expenses.
- **Example:**
    - Monthly expenses: ₹ 50,000
    - Emergency fund needed: ₹ 3 lakh
    - Best place to save: High-interest savings account or liquid mutual funds.

Case Study:
Ramesh, a freelancer, used his emergency fund to manage expenses during the pandemic.

Step 3: Save for a House

Amit: "We want to buy a house in 5 years. What's the plan?"

Rohan: "Let's calculate the down payment."

- **House cost:** ₹ 50 lakh
- **Down payment (20%):** ₹ 10 lakh
- **Plan:**
    - Invest ₹ 15,000/month in a balanced mutual fund.
    - Expected return: 10% per year.

Result:
After 5 years, ₹ 15,000/month grows to ₹ 11 lakh, covering your down payment.

Step 4: Plan for Your Daughter's Education

Priya: "How can we save for our daughter's college education in 10 years?"

Rohan: "Education costs rise with inflation. Plan accordingly."

- **Current cost:** ☐ 10 lakh
- **Future cost (after 10 years):** About ☐ 20 lakh
- **Plan:**
    - Invest ☐ 12,000/month in an equity mutual fund.
    - Expected return: 12% per year.

Result:
In 10 years, ☐ 12,000/month grows to ☐ 23 lakh, enough for her education.

Example:
Kavita saved consistently for her son's education and had ☐ 20 lakh ready when he joined IIT.

Step 5: Plan for Retirement

Amit: "Retirement seems far away, but we know we need to start early."

Rohan: "The sooner you start, the better."

- **Today's monthly expenses:** ☐ 50,000
- **Future expenses (in 20 years with inflation):** ☐ 2 lakh/month
- **Retirement fund needed:** ☐ 5 crore
- **Plan:**
    - Invest ☐ 20,000/month in a diversified equity fund.
    - Expected return: 12% per year.

Result:
In 20 years, ₹20,000/month grows to ₹3.8 crore. Combine with PPF, NPS, and EPF to reach ₹5 crore.

Example:
Ramesh, a government employee, invested in NPS and retired with ₹2 crore, ensuring a comfortable future.

Tools for Financial Planning

Rohan's Recommendations:

- **SIP Calculators:** Groww, Zerodha, Moneycontrol
- **Budgeting Apps:** Walnut, ET Money
- **Portfolio Trackers:** INDmoney, Smallcase

Key Takeaways

1. **Set Clear Goals:** Know your short-term, medium-term, and long-term goals.
2. **Diversify Investments:** Balance SIPs, mutual funds, PPFs, and other tools.
3. **Review Regularly:** Adjust your plan as life changes.

Reflection Question

"Are your current savings aligned with your future goals?"

Next Chapter Preview

Chapter 11: Protecting Wealth — Insurance & Risk Management
Learn how to safeguard your hard-earned wealth from unexpected risks.

Chapter 11: "Protecting Wealth"
Insurance & Risk Management

The Importance of Insurance

Amit and Priya meet Rohan at their usual café. Priya looks worried.

Priya: "One of my colleagues had an accident last week. His family is struggling. What if something happens to us?"
Rohan: "That's why insurance is crucial. Think of it as a safety net. You hope you never need it, but it's there if you do."

What is Insurance?

Rohan explains:
"Insurance transfers risk from you to an insurance company. If something unexpected happens, the insurer helps you financially."

Types of Insurance

There are different types of insurance, each protecting a specific aspect of your life:

1. **Life Insurance** – Protects your family if you pass away.
2. **Health Insurance** – Covers medical expenses.
3. **Motor Insurance** – Protects your car and others on the road.
4. **Home Insurance** – Protects your house from damage or theft.
5. **Critical Illness & Disability Insurance** – Covers serious illnesses or disabilities.

1. Life Insurance: Securing Your Family's Future

Purpose: Provides financial support to your family if you pass away.

Types:

- **Term Insurance:**
    - Pure protection with a low premium and high cover.
    - Example: ☐ 1 crore cover for just ☐ 10,000 per year.
    - **Tip:** Best for maximum coverage at a low cost.
- **Endowment & ULIPs:**
    - Combine insurance with investment but have lower cover and higher premiums.
    - **Caution:** Don't mix insurance with investment.

Real-Life Example:
Anand, 35, bought a term plan. When he passed away, his family received ☐ 1 crore. This helped cover his kids' education and his wife's expenses.

---

2. Health Insurance: Protecting Against Medical Costs

Priya: "Medical costs are so high. What should we look for in health insurance?"
Rohan: "Health insurance is essential. It protects your savings from expensive medical bills."

Choosing the Right Health Insurance:

1. **Coverage Amount:** At least ☐ 5 lakh for a family of four.
2. **Type:** Individual plans, family floaters, or critical illness cover.
3. **Check:**
    - Room rent limits
    - Pre-existing disease cover
    - Claim settlement ratio

Example:
Manisha's health policy covered ₹12 lakh for her cancer treatment, saving her family from financial stress.

Extra Tip:

- **Top-Up Plans:** Add extra coverage at a lower cost.

---

3. Motor & Home Insurance: Safeguarding Assets

Motor Insurance:

- Mandatory in India. Covers car damage and third-party liability.
- **Example:** Ajay's ₹1 lakh car repair was fully covered by insurance.

Home Insurance:

- Protects your house from fire, theft, or natural disasters.
- **Example:** Seema's home insurance covered ₹10 lakh after flood damage.

---

4. Critical Illness & Disability Insurance: Preparing for the Worst

Purpose: Provides a lump sum if diagnosed with serious illnesses like cancer or if disabled.

- **Example:** ₹20 lakh cover for just ₹4,000/year.

Case Study:
Arun's critical illness policy payout covered his medical bills and income loss when he was diagnosed with a heart condition.

How Much Insurance Do You Need?

Rohan: "Let's calculate your insurance needs."

1. **Life Insurance:**
    - Formula: **Annual Expenses × 10 + Loans + Future Goals**
    - Example: ☐ 5 lakh/year expenses × 10 = ☐ 50 lakh cover.
    - Add ☐ 20 lakh for loans and ☐ 30 lakh for education = ☐ 1 crore total cover.
2. **Health Insurance:**
    - For a family of four, aim for ☐ 10-15 lakh coverage.

Avoid Common Mistakes

1. **Underinsuring:** Not having enough coverage.
2. **Overlapping Policies:** Avoid buying multiple policies with similar coverage.
3. **Ignoring the Fine Print:** Understand what is and isn't covered.

Key Takeaways

1. **Insurance = Protection, Not Investment:** Focus on adequate coverage.
2. **Review Policies Regularly:** Update as your life changes (marriage, kids, loans).
3. **Be Prepared:** Insurance ensures financial stability during crises.

Reflection Question:

"Do you have enough insurance to protect your family's future and assets?"

Next Chapter Preview:

Chapter 12: Beating Inflation — Advanced Investment Strategies
Learn how to ensure your investments grow faster than inflation!

Chapter 12: "Beating Inflation" Advanced Investment Strategies

A Wake-Up Call:

In a coffee shop, Meera is talking to her friend Rishi about her frustration with inflation.

Meera: "I've been saving diligently in my bank account, but my savings don't seem to be growing. Every year, it feels like the money I saved is worth less. What should I do?"
Rishi: "The problem is inflation. Saving money in the bank won't cut it. To truly grow your wealth, you need to invest in assets that outpace inflation."

Understanding Inflation and Investment:

Rishi explains:
"Inflation is the increase in the price of goods and services over time. If inflation is 6% annually, the value of your money decreases by that percentage each year. So, if you keep ☐ 1 lakh in your bank account at 3% interest, your actual returns are negative when you factor in inflation."

Real-Life Example:

Case Study:

Meera has ☐ 1,00,000 in her bank account, earning 3% interest. But inflation is at 6%.

Calculation:

- Interest earned = ☐ 3,000 (☐ 1,00,000 × 3%)
- Inflation loss = ☐ 6,000 (☐ 1,00,000 × 6%)
- Real return = ☐ 3,000 − ☐ 6,000 = -☐ **3,000**

Rishi continues:
"That's why traditional savings accounts aren't enough. You need investments that give you returns higher than inflation."

Advanced Investment Strategies to Beat Inflation:

Rishi: "There are several investment options that can help you beat inflation. Let's go through them one by one."

1. Stocks and Equity Mutual Funds — The Power of the Market

Rishi: "Equity has historically outpaced inflation. Stocks and equity mutual funds can offer returns higher than the average inflation rate over the long term."

Why Stocks Beat Inflation:

Stocks represent ownership in companies that grow over time, passing on profits to shareholders.

Historically, the stock market has provided long-term returns of **12-15% annually**, significantly higher than inflation.

Example:

Case Study:

Rajesh invested ☐ 10,000 in an index fund tracking the Nifty 50 (India's top 50 companies) for 20 years.

Average return: 12% annually.

Growth: ☐ 10,000 grew to ☐ 96,000.

Inflation-adjusted return: Even after accounting for an average 6% inflation, Rajesh's investment grew significantly, preserving and increasing his purchasing power.

Important Tip:

If you're not sure where to start, you can invest in **Index Funds** or **ETFs** (Exchange-Traded Funds), which automatically diversify your investment across several stocks.

2. Real Estate — A Tangible Asset

Rishi: "Real estate is another excellent hedge against inflation. Property values tend to rise over time due to increasing demand and limited supply."

Why Real Estate Beats Inflation:

Appreciation: Real estate generally appreciates in value, outpacing inflation.

Rental Income: In times of high inflation, rental income can increase, protecting against rising costs.

Example:

Case Study:

Sunil bought a flat in 2010 for ☐ 30 lakh.

By 2023, the flat's market value had risen to ☐ 75 lakh, a 150% increase.

Rental income: ☐ 25,000 per month, which also increased over time.

Real-Life Tip:

Buy properties in emerging locations or cities where demand is growing, or invest in **Real Estate Investment Trusts (REITs)** if you want to invest in real estate without buying property.

3. Gold — The Ancient Hedge

Rishi: "Gold has been a store of value for thousands of years. During periods of high inflation or economic uncertainty, gold often retains or increases in value."

Why Gold Beats Inflation:

Gold is a finite resource, and its value tends to rise when inflation and global uncertainties increase.

Gold can be a stable addition to a diversified investment portfolio.

Example:

Case Study:

Sonia bought 1 kg of gold in 2011 at ☐ 25,000.

By 2023, the price of gold rose to ☐ 55,000 per gram, and her gold was worth ☐ 55 lakh, more than double its value.

Additional Tip:

Invest in gold through **Gold ETFs** or **Sovereign Gold Bonds** to avoid the hassle of physical storage.

4. Bonds and Fixed Income Instruments — Stability with Returns

Rishi: "Bonds are a safer investment than stocks, providing fixed returns over time. While bonds may not offer the explosive growth of stocks, they provide stability and a steady income."

Why Bonds Help Combat Inflation?

While bonds offer fixed returns, many government bonds or corporate bonds tend to outperform inflation, especially if interest rates rise.

Some bonds are inflation-linked, such as **Inflation-Linked Bonds (ILBs)**, which offer returns directly tied to inflation.

Example:

Case Study:

Neha invested ☐ 5 lakh in an inflation-linked bond offering 6% return plus inflation.

If inflation was 5%, her total return for the year would be 11%, providing a good buffer against inflation.

5. Systematic Investment Plans (SIPs)

Rishi: "SIPs are an excellent way to beat inflation because they allow you to invest regularly in mutual funds. Over time, the value of your SIP grows, compounding your returns and beating inflation."

Why SIPs Help:

SIPs allow you to invest small amounts regularly, taking advantage of **rupee cost averaging**.

Over time, they benefit from market growth, and the compounding effect helps your wealth grow faster than inflation.

Example:

Case Study:

Simran invested ₹5,000 monthly in a mutual fund via SIP for 10 years.

At an average return of 12% annually, her ₹5,000 monthly investment grew to ₹11.6 lakh. Even with inflation of 6%, her wealth increased by more than ₹6 lakh.

Creating a Diversified Portfolio:

Rishi: "The key to beating inflation is diversification. Don't put all your eggs in one basket. A mix of stocks, bonds, real estate, gold, and SIPs creates a balanced portfolio that can withstand inflation and economic uncertainty."

Real-Life Example:

Case Study:

Karan divided his ₹10 lakh investment as follows:

- ₹4 lakh in stocks and equity funds
- ₹3 lakh in real estate
- ₹1 lakh in gold
- ₹2 lakh in bonds

Over 10 years, his portfolio grew by 10-12% annually, comfortably outpacing inflation.

Key Takeaways:

1. **Don't Rely on Savings Accounts Alone:** They won't keep up with inflation.
2. **Invest in Stocks and Mutual Funds:** Historically, they beat inflation over time.
3. **Consider Real Estate and Gold:** These tangible assets hold their value and protect your wealth.

4. **Diversify Your Investments:** Spread your money across multiple asset classes to reduce risk and maximize returns.
5. **Use SIPs for Regular Investments:** They help you take advantage of market growth while minimizing risk.

Reflection Question:

"Are your investments beating inflation, or is your money losing value in a savings account?"

Next Chapter Preview:

Chapter 13: The Final Frontier — Tax Planning and Maximizing Your Returns
Learn how tax-efficient strategies can further increase your savings and ensure that your wealth continues to grow without unnecessary taxation.

Chapter 13: "The Final Frontier"

Tax Planning and Maximizing Your Returns

The Hidden Cost of Taxes:

In a bustling café, Priya and Aarav are discussing their investment strategies.

Priya: "I've made some good returns from my stocks and SIPs, but my returns are always lower than I expect. I'm paying a lot in taxes, and it feels like I'm losing half of it."

Aarav: "That's the hidden cost of not planning your taxes. Taxes can eat into your wealth over time, but with proper planning, you can minimize them and maximize your returns."

The Impact of Taxes on Your Wealth:

Aarav explains:
"Taxes are a necessary part of our economy, but they can be a major drag on your investments if you don't plan for them. The more you earn, the more you pay in taxes — and that can significantly reduce the compound effect of your investments."

Real-Life Example:

Case Study:

Ravi earned ₹ 10,00,000 in capital gains from stocks in one year.

Without tax planning, he paid **15% tax** on the gain, which amounted to ₹ 1,50,000.

After tax, his net gain was ₹ 8,50,000, reducing his return significantly.

Understanding Different Types of Taxes:

Aarav: "Let's break down the major taxes that affect your savings and investments."

Income Tax

This is the tax you pay on your earnings from salary, business income, and other sources. The tax rate varies based on your income bracket.

Tax Brackets in India (FY 2023-24):

- ₹ 0 – ₹ 2.5 lakh: No tax
- ₹ 2.5 lakh – ₹ 5 lakh: 5%
- ₹ 5 lakh – ₹ 10 lakh: 20%
- ₹ 10 lakh and above: 30%

Real-Life Example:

Sanjay earns ₹ 12,00,000 annually. His tax calculation is:

- First ₹ 2.5 lakh: **No tax**
- Next ₹ 2.5 lakh: **5% tax = ₹ 12,500**
- Next ₹ 5 lakh: **20% tax = ₹ 1,00,000**
- Remaining ₹ 2 lakh: **30% tax = ₹ 60,000**

Total tax: ₹ 1,72,500

Capital Gains Tax

Short-Term Capital Gains (STCG): If you sell assets like stocks or mutual funds within 3 years of buying, the gains are taxed at **15%** for equity investments.

Long-Term Capital Gains (LTCG): If you hold assets for more than 3 years, the gains are taxed at **10%** if they exceed ₹1 lakh in a year (for equities).

Example:

Aman sold stocks for ₹5 lakh after holding them for 2 years.

He paid **15% STCG tax** on the ₹1 lakh gain, amounting to ₹15,000.

Dividend Tax

Dividends from stocks or mutual funds are also taxed.

Tax on Dividends: If the dividend income exceeds ₹5,000, it is taxed at **10%**.

Example:

Maya received ₹7,000 in dividends from her mutual fund.

She paid **10% tax**, which amounts to ₹700.

Tax-Saving Instruments — How to Maximize Your Returns:

Aarav: "Now, let's talk about how you can save on taxes while growing your wealth."

Section 80C — The Tax-Saving Superpower

Section 80C of the Income Tax Act allows you to invest in certain instruments and reduce your taxable income by up to ☐ 1.5 lakh annually.

Eligible Investments:

- **Public Provident Fund (PPF)**
- **Employee Provident Fund (EPF)**
- **National Savings Certificates (NSC)**
- **Tax-Saving Fixed Deposits**
- **ELSS (Equity-Linked Savings Scheme) Mutual Funds**

Real-Life Example:

Neeraji invests ☐ 1.5 lakh in an ELSS mutual fund under Section 80C.

His taxable income is reduced by ☐ 1.5 lakh, lowering his tax liability for the year.

National Pension Scheme (NPS) — Additional Tax Savings

You can also claim an additional deduction of ☐ 50,000 under **Section 80CCD(1B)** for contributions to the NPS. This is over and above the ☐ 1.5 lakh limit under Section 80C.

NPS investments not only save taxes but also help you build a retirement corpus.

Example:

Rajeev contributes ☐ 50,000 to the NPS.

He claims a tax deduction of ☐ 50,000, further reducing his taxable income.

Tax-Efficient Mutual Funds

Index Funds and **ETFs** often have lower turnover, which results in lower capital gains tax liability compared to actively managed funds.

Long-term investments in tax-efficient funds can significantly reduce the tax burden.

Real Estate — Tax Benefits on Home Loans

If you take a home loan, you can claim deductions under **Section 80C** (up to ₹ 1.5 lakh) on principal repayment and **Section 24(b)** (up to ₹ 2 lakh) on interest payments.

Example:

Priya took a home loan for ₹ 30 lakh, and she paid ₹ 1.2 lakh as principal and ₹ 2 lakh as interest in a financial year.

She can claim a total tax deduction of ₹ 3.2 lakh.

Creating a Tax-Efficient Portfolio:

Aarav: "The goal is to create a portfolio that not only generates good returns but also helps minimize your tax liability. Here's how you can do it."

Maximize Tax-Advantaged Accounts

Contribute the maximum amount allowed to Section 80C instruments and NPS to reduce taxable income.

Use tax-efficient mutual funds like index funds or ETFs to minimize long-term capital gains taxes.

Long-Term Investment Strategy

Hold investments for the long term to take advantage of **LTCG** tax benefits and reduce short-term taxes.

Reinvest dividends to avoid taxes on them annually and allow your money to compound.

Diversify Your Investments

Diversify your portfolio across stocks, bonds, mutual funds, and real estate to optimize returns and spread out tax liabilities.

Use Tax Loss Harvesting

Tax-loss harvesting involves selling investments that have declined in value to offset gains in other areas, thus reducing the taxable amount. This can be a useful strategy to lower your capital gains taxes.

A Real-Life Example of Tax Efficiency:

Aarav: "Let's look at how tax-efficient planning can change your wealth-building journey."

Case Study:

Nisha invested ☐ 1.5 lakh in an ELSS mutual fund under Section 80C.

She also invested ☐ 50,000 in NPS for additional tax savings.

Over 10 years, her investments grew at an annual rate of 12%.

Without tax planning, her returns would have been taxed heavily, but by using tax-saving instruments, she reduced her tax burden by nearly ☐ 2 lakh over the years.

Key Takeaways:

1. **Taxes Can Eat Into Your Wealth:** Understand the types of taxes that affect your income and investments.
2. **Use Tax-Saving Instruments:** Invest in Section 80C, NPS, and other tax-efficient tools to reduce your taxable income.
3. **Maximize Long-Term Capital Gains:** Hold investments for longer periods to minimize capital gains taxes.
4. **Create a Diversified and Tax-Efficient Portfolio:** Mix tax-saving instruments with growth assets to build wealth efficiently.
5. **Consider Tax Loss Harvesting:** Offset capital gains by selling losing investments to reduce tax liabilities.

Reflection Question:

"Are you actively using tax-saving strategies to maximize your returns and minimize your tax burden?"

Next Chapter Preview:

Chapter 14: Creating a Financial Safety Net — Emergency Funds and Insurance
Learn why building an emergency fund and securing insurance coverage is crucial for long-term financial security, and how to prepare for the unexpected.

Chapter 14: "Creating a Financial Safety Net"

Emergency Funds and Insurance

The Unpredictable Storm:

In a small café in the city, Neha and Karan were catching up after work.
Neha: "Last month, I lost my job. It came as such a shock! I didn't even have enough savings to last a month."
Karan: "That's why you need an emergency fund. Life is unpredictable. Emergencies, whether it's a job loss, medical expenses, or unforeseen repairs, can happen at any time."

The Importance of an Emergency Fund:

Karan explains:
"An emergency fund is a financial safety net that covers unexpected expenses without derailing your long-term financial goals. Without it, you might be forced to dip into your investments or take on debt in a crisis."

Real-Life Example:

Case Study:
Amit had an emergency fund of ☐ 5 lakh, which he had built over two years. When his car broke down and he needed an urgent medical procedure, he was able to pay for everything from his emergency fund.

Without the emergency fund, he would have needed to take out a loan or sell investments at a loss.

How Much Should You Save in Your Emergency Fund?

Karan continues:
"The size of your emergency fund depends on your monthly expenses and lifestyle. A good rule of thumb is to save enough to cover at least 3 to 6 months of living expenses."

If You Have Dependents or a Mortgage:
Aim for 6 months of expenses, as you may need more time to recover financially.
If You Are Single or Have Lower Expenses:
3 to 4 months might be sufficient.

Example:
Rina calculates her monthly expenses, including rent, groceries, utilities, and entertainment.

- Monthly Expenses: ☐ 50,000
- Emergency Fund Goal: ☐ 50,000 × 6 = ☐ 3,00,000
  Rina sets up an SIP in a liquid mutual fund and systematically invests to build her emergency fund.

Where to Keep Your Emergency Fund?

Karan: "It's important to store your emergency fund somewhere it's accessible but still earns some returns. That means avoiding investing it in risky stocks or bonds."

High-Interest Savings Accounts:
Some banks offer high-interest savings accounts that provide better returns than regular accounts while still keeping your money liquid.

Liquid Mutual Funds:
These are low-risk funds that can be easily accessed when needed. They offer higher returns than a savings account.

Fixed Deposits (FDs):
While not as liquid as savings accounts, FDs offer guaranteed returns and are a safe place to park your emergency fund.

The Role of Insurance in Financial Safety:

Karan: "The second part of your safety net is insurance. Insurance protects you from financial losses in case of medical emergencies, accidents, or even death."

Real-Life Example:

Case Study:
Deepak had health insurance that covered his family's medical expenses during a critical surgery. He didn't need to dip into his savings or emergency fund, as his insurance covered 80% of the medical bills. If Deepak had not had insurance, he would have been forced to take out a loan or liquidate his investments.

Types of Insurance You Need:

Health Insurance:
This is a must-have, especially in today's world where medical expenses are soaring. Ensure you have adequate coverage that covers hospitalization, surgeries, and critical illnesses.
Example:
Manoji has a health insurance policy for ☐ 5 lakh, which covers his family's medical expenses. When his wife required an urgent surgery, the policy covered all expenses, and Manoj didn't need to worry about the costs.

Life Insurance:
If you have dependents, a life insurance policy can ensure that they are financially protected in the event of your untimely death. Consider a term insurance plan that provides a high sum assured for a relatively low premium.

Example:
Vinay purchased a term life insurance plan for ₹ 50 lakh with a low premium. In the unfortunate event of his death, his family received the insurance payout, which ensured their financial security.

Disability Insurance:
Disability insurance provides income replacement if you become disabled and are unable to work. This is particularly important for those whose income is heavily reliant on their ability to work.

Car Insurance:
Car insurance is mandatory in many countries. It protects you financially in case of accidents, damage, or theft. Always ensure you have comprehensive coverage to protect against a variety of risks.

Building a Robust Safety Net:

Karan: "Now, let's look at how to build a complete safety net."

Start with Your Emergency Fund:
Assess your monthly expenses and start setting aside money for your emergency fund. Keep it in a liquid, low-risk instrument, such as a high-interest savings account or a liquid mutual fund.

Get Adequate Insurance Coverage:
Buy health insurance for yourself and your family. If you have dependents, ensure you have life insurance coverage that will replace your income if something happens to you. Consider additional coverage like disability insurance if your work depends on your health and ability to work.

Revisit Your Safety Net Regularly:
Your life situation will change over time. As your income increases, review your insurance and emergency fund to ensure they remain adequate. Periodically assess your health insurance and life insurance coverage to ensure it meets your current needs.

Real-Life Example of a Strong Safety Net:

Case Study:
Priya and Anil were a young couple with two children. They set aside ☐ 3,00,000 for an emergency fund, which was sufficient to cover 6 months of expenses. Priya took out a health insurance policy for ☐ 10 lakh, while Anil bought a term life insurance policy for ☐ 50 lakh. When Priya was hospitalized due to a medical emergency, their health insurance covered 90% of the cost. Anil's life insurance ensured that if anything happened to him, Priya and the kids would be financially secure.

Creating a Financial Safety Net for the Future:

Karan: "The key takeaway is that life is uncertain, and being prepared for unexpected events can make all the difference in maintaining your financial well-being. By setting up an emergency fund and securing the right insurance, you're building a solid foundation for your financial future."

Key Takeaways:

1. **An Emergency Fund is Essential:** It covers unexpected expenses like medical emergencies, job loss, or home repairs.

2. **Save 3 to 6 Months' Expenses:** Aim to have enough to cover 3-6 months of living expenses, depending on your lifestyle and dependents.
3. **Choose Liquid, Safe Investment Options:** High-interest savings accounts, liquid mutual funds, and fixed deposits are great places to park your emergency fund.
4. **Insurance Protects Against Financial Losses:** Health, life, disability, and car insurance are essential components of your financial safety net.
5. **Regularly Review Your Coverage:** As your life changes, ensure your emergency fund and insurance policies reflect your current needs.

Reflection Question:

"Do you have a solid financial safety net in place to handle unexpected situations, or do you need to start building one today?"

Next Chapter Preview:

Chapter 15: The Road to Financial Independence — Setting Long-Term Goals
Discover how setting clear long-term financial goals and breaking them into actionable steps can lead you to financial freedom. We'll also explore retirement planning, building wealth over time, and achieving your dreams.

Chapter 15: "The Road to Financial Independence"

Setting Long-Term Goals

Dreaming Big with Vision:

At a cozy café, Neha and Karan are once again in conversation, this time discussing their future goals.

Neha: "I've been thinking a lot about the future lately. Everyone keeps talking about financial freedom, but I don't know where to start."
Karan: "That's the first step — realizing the importance of long-term goals. Financial freedom doesn't happen overnight. But with clear vision and planning, you can achieve it. Let me show you how to set goals that will bring you closer to financial independence."

What is Financial Independence?

Karan explains:
"Financial independence means having enough income from your investments and savings to cover your living expenses without relying on a job or active work. It's about creating a life where money doesn't control you, but instead, you control your money."

Real-Life Example:

Case Study:

Sandeep started working in his 20s with the goal of financial independence by the time he turned 45. He followed a disciplined savings strategy, invested in equities, and built multiple passive income streams.

By 45, Sandeep had accumulated enough assets to live off the returns of his investments, achieving financial independence. He continued to work for passion, not necessity.

Why Setting Long-Term Financial Goals is Important?

Karan:
"When you set long-term financial goals, you're giving your financial life direction. Without goals, you're like a ship without a rudder, drifting wherever the waves of inflation, unexpected expenses, and lifestyle changes take you."

Defining Clear Milestones:
Setting goals provides measurable milestones that keep you motivated and on track. It's easy to get lost when you don't know where you're headed.

Aligning Your Savings and Investments:
Your long-term goals shape your savings and investment decisions. When you have a clear target, you can choose the right investment vehicles, whether that's real estate, stocks, or mutual funds.

SMART Goals — The Foundation of Financial Independence:

Karan: "To set effective goals, you should follow the SMART criteria. SMART goals are: Specific, Measurable, Achievable, Relevant, and Time-bound."

Specific:

Be clear about what you want to achieve. For example, instead of "I want to save more money," say, "I want to save ☐ 10 lakh for my retirement by the time I'm 50."

Measurable:

Set a clear target. This allows you to track progress. For example, "Save ☐ 5,000 every month" is measurable.

Achievable:

Make sure your goal is realistic. Don't overburden yourself. If saving ☐ 50,000 every month isn't possible, aim for a smaller amount that's more in line with your current financial capacity.

Relevant:

Your goals should align with your long-term objectives. For example, if you're aiming for retirement, then your goal should relate to building wealth for that specific purpose.

Time-bound:

Set a deadline for achieving the goal. For example, "I want to accumulate ☐ 10 lakh by 5 years from now."

Breaking Down Your Financial Goals into Actionable Steps:

Karan:
"Now, let's break down your big goal into smaller, actionable steps. This is where most people go wrong—they think of financial independence as a distant dream, but they never plan the steps to reach it."

Example of Setting Long-Term Financial Goals:

Neha: "Okay, let's take retirement as an example. How should I plan for it?"

Karan:
"Let's say you want to retire with ₹1 crore in 20 years. To get there, break it down like this:"

Step 1: Determine your current savings. Let's assume you have ₹5 lakh saved up.

Step 2: Calculate how much you need to save each year to reach your goal.

To accumulate ₹1 crore in 20 years, you'll need to save about ₹1.25 lakh per year (excluding investment growth).

Step 3: Invest the amount in a combination of **equities** (for long-term growth) and **debt funds** (for stability).

Understanding the Power of Compound Interest:

Karan:
"Once you've broken down your goal, the next thing you need to understand is the power of compound interest."

Example:

Ravi's Investment in Mutual Funds:

Ravi invests ₹10,000 every month in a mutual fund that gives him an average annual return of 12%.

In **10 years**, his ₹12 lakh investment (₹10,000 × 12 × 10) grows to ₹30.4 lakh, thanks to the power of compound interest. The longer your investment horizon, the more compound interest works in your favor.

Building Multiple Streams of Income:

Karan:
"Financial independence is often achieved through multiple streams of income. Relying on one income source (usually your salary) isn't enough, especially in today's volatile world."

Real Estate Investment:

Example:

Sanjay invested in a rental property that provided him a steady stream of passive income.

Over time, as property prices appreciated, his net worth grew significantly.

Stocks and Mutual Funds:

Dividends and capital gains from stocks and mutual funds can provide additional income.

Example:

Neha invested in stocks that paid quarterly dividends. These dividends acted as additional income that helped her save for her children's education.

Side Businesses:

Running a small side business like freelancing, tutoring, or an online store can help boost your income.

Retirement Planning and Early Financial Independence:

Karan:
"Retirement planning is one of the most crucial long-term financial goals. The earlier you start, the better it is. Many people wait until their 40s or 50s to think about retirement, but it's never too early to start."

Real-Life Example:

Case Study:

Priya started contributing ₹ 10,000 to her EPF (Employees' Provident Fund) and PPF (Public Provident Fund) in her 20s.

By the time she reached 50, she had accumulated ₹ 30 lakh from her PPF, ₹ 10 lakh from her EPF, and ₹ 20 lakh from her SIPs in equity funds.

With consistent contributions and the magic of compounding, Priya achieved financial independence much earlier than expected.

Monitoring and Adjusting Your Goals:

Karan:
"Finally, don't forget that your financial goals aren't set in stone. Life will change, and so will your goals."

Example:

Ajay had originally set his retirement goal at ₹ 1 crore. However, after buying a house and starting a family, he adjusted his target to ₹ 2 crore.

He increased his savings rate and adjusted his investments to meet this new goal.

Key Takeaways:

1. **Financial Independence is Achievable:** With clear goals and disciplined saving and investing, you can achieve financial freedom.

2. **Use SMART Goals:** Make sure your financial goals are Specific, Measurable, Achievable, Relevant, and Time-bound.
3. **Compound Interest is Powerful:** Starting early and investing consistently helps your money grow exponentially.
4. **Create Multiple Streams of Income:** Diversify your income sources for financial security.
5. **Regularly Review and Adjust Your Goals:** Life changes, and so should your financial goals.

Reflection Question:

"What are your long-term financial goals, and how will you break them down into actionable steps to achieve financial independence?"

Next Chapter Preview:

Chapter 16: Managing Debt — The Silent Killer of Wealth
Explore the concept of good debt vs. bad debt, and learn how to manage and eliminate debt to build a solid financial future.

Chapter 16: "Managing Debt"
The Silent Killer of Wealth

The Weight of Debt:

In a busy local market, Neha is catching up with an old friend, Arjun, who is troubled.

Neha: "Hey Arjun, you don't look your usual energetic self. What's been going on?"
Arjun: "It's this constant pressure. I've been paying off one loan after another. The EMIs just keep piling up, and I feel stuck. Every month, a large portion of my income goes into paying these debts."
Neha: "I know how you feel. I've been reading a lot about managing debt and how it can really affect your financial health. Let me share what I've learned."

Understanding Debt — Good vs. Bad Debt:

Neha explains:
"Debt isn't always bad. There's a difference between 'good debt' and 'bad debt'. The key knows how to use debt to your advantage."

Good Debt:
Good debt is used to finance investments that will generate returns over time, such as education, business loans, or real estate. The returns from these investments typically outweigh the interest you pay on the debt.

Example:

Rajesh took a loan to pursue an MBA, which helped him secure a high-paying job, doubling his income in a few years. The interest on the loan was far less than the increased income he generated from his education.

Bad Debt:
Bad debt is typically used for consumables, or expenses that don't appreciate in value, like credit card debt, personal loans for vacations, or car loans for luxury items. This type of debt doesn't help you build wealth, and the interest often compounds, eating into your finances.

Example:

Sanjay took a personal loan for a foreign vacation. While it was an enjoyable trip, the loan's interest rate was high, and it took him years to pay it off, without any long-term benefit to his financial health.

How Debt Affects Your Financial Freedom:

Arjun: "I always thought I could just manage my debts by paying the minimum EMI. I didn't realize how much they were holding me back."
Neha: "That's the thing. Debt isn't just about the amount you owe; it's also about the interest and the long-term impact it has on your savings and investments. When you're in debt, you're paying for past consumption, which means your money isn't being used to build your wealth."

Real-Life Example:

Example of Compound Debt:

Nina had ☐ 1 lakh in credit card debt with an interest rate of 18% per year.

Over the course of 2 years, if Nina only made the minimum payments, her debt would balloon, increasing the total amount she owes.

Instead of growing her savings, she'd be stuck in a cycle of paying interest.

The Debt Trap — When Payments Keep You Stuck:

Neha:
"Here's the problem with debt: as you keep paying off your minimum EMIs, your progress towards becoming debt-free is incredibly slow. The interest eats away at your ability to build wealth."

Example:

Vikram's Car Loan:

Vikram took out a ☐ 5 lakh car loan with a 10% interest rate for 5 years.

Although he made regular payments, the interest meant that, after 3 years, he had paid ☐ 1.5 lakh in interest, but still owed ☐ 3 lakh on the car loan.

This was a huge drain on his savings and meant he had less money to invest elsewhere.

Strategies to Manage Debt Effectively:

Neha: "The key is to manage debt wisely and reduce it as quickly as possible. Here are some effective strategies to do that."

Debt Snowball Method:

Focus on paying off your smallest debts first while making minimum payments on the larger ones. Once the smaller debt is cleared, move on to the next, gaining momentum with each payment.

Example:

Karan had three debts: a ₹ 10,000 credit card balance, a ₹ 50,000 personal loan, and a ₹ 1 lakh car loan.

He paid off the credit card balance first, then focused on the personal loan, and finally, cleared the car loan.

Each time a debt was paid off, he felt a sense of accomplishment, and it motivated him to tackle the next debt with more intensity.

Debt Avalanche Method:

Prioritize paying off the debt with the highest interest rate first. This method saves you more money in the long run by minimizing interest payments.

Example:

Shalini had two debts: a ₹ 50,000 personal loan at 15% interest and ₹ 1 lakh in student loans at 8%.

Using the debt avalanche method, she focused on clearing the higher-interest personal loan first, reducing the total interest she would pay over time.

Consolidating Debt:

If you have multiple high-interest debts, consider consolidating them into one loan with a lower interest rate. This can simplify your payments and reduce your overall interest burden.

Example:

Ravi consolidated his credit card debt, personal loan, and car loan into a single loan with a 10% interest rate, down from a combined 18%.

This made his payments easier to manage and saved him money on interest.

Avoiding the Debt Trap — Building Healthy Financial Habits:

Neha: "Now, let's talk about how to avoid falling into the debt trap in the first place. Building healthy financial habits is crucial."

Live Below Your Means:

One of the simplest ways to avoid debt is to avoid spending more than you earn. Creating a budget, tracking your expenses, and distinguishing between needs and wants can help you control your spending.

Emergency Fund:

Having an emergency fund helps you avoid taking on debt for unforeseen expenses. Aim to save 3–6 months of living expenses in an easily accessible account.

Use Credit Responsibly:

Credit cards can be useful for building credit and earning rewards, but avoid carrying balances. Pay off the full amount each month to avoid high-interest charges.

The Road to Becoming Debt-Free:

Neha: "Once you get rid of debt, the next step is to stay debt-free and continue to build wealth."

Example:

Nisha's Debt-Free Journey:

Nisha paid off her credit card and personal loans in 2 years using the debt snowball method.

After becoming debt-free, she redirected her monthly EMI payments into mutual fund investments.

Over the next 5 years, her investments grew significantly, providing her with the financial freedom to start her own business.

The Power of Financial Discipline

Neha:
"Debt is a silent killer of wealth. But with the right strategies, you can manage and eliminate it. Once you free yourself from debt, you'll have more control over your money, and that's when you can focus on building real wealth."

Key Takeaways:

1. **Good Debt vs. Bad Debt:**
   Understand the difference between good debt (investments that appreciate) and bad debt (loans for consumables).
2. **Debt Snowball vs. Debt Avalanche:**
   Choose the right strategy for clearing your debt. The debt snowball offers psychological wins, while the debt avalanche saves money in interest.
3. **Consolidating Debt:**
   Consolidate high-interest debts to reduce your overall interest burden.
4. **Healthy Financial Habits:**
   Build an emergency fund, live below your means, and use credit responsibly to avoid falling into the debt trap.

Reflection Question:

"What steps will you take today to reduce your debt and build a healthier financial future?"

Next Chapter Preview:

Chapter 17: Overcoming Inflation with Smart Investments
Explore how to use smart investments to combat inflation and preserve your wealth for the future.

Chapter 17: "Overcoming Inflation"
Smart Investments

Understanding the Power of Inflation:

At a local café, Sameer and Priya are sipping their coffee while discussing their finances. Sameer is worried about the rising costs of daily essentials.

Sameer: "Priya, have you noticed how everything is becoming so expensive? My groceries, fuel, even the small luxuries I used to enjoy, are all costing me more. I feel like my savings are just not keeping up with inflation."

Priya: "You're not alone, Sameer. Inflation is silently eroding the value of your savings. But don't worry—there are ways to protect your wealth against inflation. Let me explain."

What is Inflation?

Priya explains:
"Inflation is the rate at which the general level of prices for goods and services rises, leading to a decrease in purchasing power. Essentially, inflation means that the money you save today will buy less in the future. If your savings are not earning more than the inflation rate, you are losing money over time."

Example:

The ☐ 10,000 Dilemma:

If you save ☐ 10,000 today and inflation is at 6%, in one year, the same ☐ 10,000 will only have the purchasing power of ☐ 9,433.

In essence, by doing nothing, you are losing ☐ 567 in value without even spending it!

The Impact of Inflation on Savings:

Sameer: "But my savings are sitting in the bank. Shouldn't that be safe from inflation?"

Priya: "That's a common misconception. While your savings may be safe in a bank, they aren't growing fast enough to beat inflation. Bank interest rates are often lower than inflation rates, which means the real value of your savings is shrinking."

Real-Life Example:

Meera's Bank Savings vs. Inflation:

Meera kept ☐ 1,00,000 in a fixed deposit at 5% annual interest.

With inflation at 7%, the real value of her ☐ 1,00,000 decreased by ☐ 2,000, even though she earned ☐ 5,000 in interest.

This shows that bank deposits may give you nominal returns, but they fail to protect against inflation over the long term.

How to Protect Against Inflation:

Priya: "So, what can you do? You need to invest your money in ways that outpace inflation. Let's talk about smart investments."

Stocks and Equities

Stocks generally provide higher returns over the long term than other asset classes and tend to outpace inflation. Investing in the stock market allows your money to grow with the economy.

Example:

Ravi's Stock Investment:

Ravi invested ₹1 lakh in an index fund that tracked the overall market. Over 10 years, the fund grew at an annual average rate of 12%.

This beat inflation (which averaged around 6%) and allowed Ravi's wealth to grow substantially.

Real Estate

Real estate is another great way to hedge against inflation. Property values tend to rise over time, and real estate also provides rental income, which can grow with inflation.

Example:

Kiran's Rental Property:

Kiran bought an apartment for ₹30 lakh a few years ago.

Over the years, property values in her area rose by 8% annually.

She was able to sell the apartment for ₹45 lakh after 5 years, gaining ₹15 lakh in capital appreciation while receiving steady rental income along the way.

Gold and Precious Metals

Gold has historically been a hedge against inflation. During periods of high inflation, the value of gold tends to rise as people seek safe assets to preserve wealth.

Example:

Asha's Investment in Gold:

Asha purchased 10 grams of gold at ₹30,000 per gram in 2015.

By 2020, the price had risen to ₹ 50,000 per gram, giving her a return of 67% over 5 years, significantly outpacing inflation.

Bonds and Fixed-Income Securities

While bonds are generally safer than stocks, inflation-linked bonds can help preserve the real value of your money. These bonds offer returns that are adjusted for inflation.

Example:

Raj's Inflation-Protected Bonds:

Raj invested ₹ 5 lakh in inflation-linked bonds that paid returns of 4% plus the inflation rate.

In an environment where inflation was 6%, Raj effectively earned 10% returns, keeping his purchasing power intact.

The Importance of Diversification:

Priya: "The key to protecting your wealth against inflation is diversification. By spreading your investments across different asset classes—stocks, bonds, real estate, and precious metals—you reduce the risk of your wealth being eroded by inflation."

Example:

Shweta's Diversified Portfolio:

Shweta invested in a balanced portfolio consisting of 50% stocks, 30% bonds, 10% gold, and 10% real estate.

Over 5 years, while inflation averaged 6%, her portfolio returned an average of 9%, ensuring her wealth grew faster than inflation.

The Power of Compounding in Beating Inflation:

Sameer: "I've heard of compounding, but how does it fit into the equation?"

Priya: "Compounding is one of the most powerful tools to fight inflation. The earlier you start investing, the more you can benefit from compounding, which is essentially earning returns on your returns."

Example:

Nikhil's Compounding Journey:

Nikhil invested ₹ 50,000 in a mutual fund that generated a 12% return annually.

After 10 years, his investment grew to ₹ 1,55,000.

By reinvesting his returns and allowing them to compound, Nikhil was able to overcome inflation and grow his wealth significantly.

How to Create an Inflation-Beating Investment Strategy:

Priya: "To create an inflation-beating investment strategy, you need to focus on long-term growth. Here are some steps to get started."

Start Early:

The sooner you start investing, the more you can take advantage of compounding returns.

Invest Regularly:

Consistent investing, such as through Systematic Investment Plans (SIPs), can help you ride out market volatility and take advantage of market dips.

Monitor Your Investments:

Regularly review your portfolio to ensure that it's performing well and adjust it based on market conditions.

The Road to Financial Freedom:

Priya: "The key to beating inflation is investing wisely and consistently. Inflation may be inevitable, but if you take proactive steps and build a diversified portfolio, you can ensure that your money works harder than inflation."

Key Takeaways:

1. **Invest in Assets That Outpace Inflation:**
   Stocks, real estate, gold, and inflation-linked bonds are some of the best ways to beat inflation.
2. **Diversify Your Investments:**
   A diversified portfolio reduces the risks of inflation eroding your wealth.
3. **Start Early and Invest Regularly:**
   The earlier you invest, the more you can benefit from compounding, which helps you grow your wealth over time.

Reflection Question:

"What steps will you take today to protect your savings from inflation?"

Next Chapter Preview:

Chapter 18: The Power of Financial Discipline — Building a Lasting Legacy
Learn how cultivating financial discipline and making mindful financial decisions can help you build a legacy that lasts for generations.

Chapter 18: "The Power of Financial Discipline"

Building a Lasting Legacy

The Importance of Financial Discipline:

At a family gathering, Rajan is talking to his father, Mr. Sharma, about his financial struggles.

Rajan: "Dad, I'm tired of living paycheck to paycheck. I want to build wealth, but I don't know where to start."
Mr. Sharma: "Rajan, the first step to building wealth is financial discipline. Without discipline, no matter how much you earn, it will always slip through your fingers. Let me tell you a story that changed my perspective on money."

The Story of Mr. Sharma's Journey:

Mr. Sharma begins recounting his early financial mistakes.

Mr. Sharma:
"When I was your age, I spent money as if it would never run out. I bought things I didn't need, spent impulsively, and lived with a 'tomorrow will take care of itself' mindset. But when inflation hit and I saw my savings being eroded, I realized something had to change. It was only when I embraced financial discipline that my situation improved."

What is Financial Discipline?

Rajan: "What do you mean by financial discipline?"
Mr. Sharma: "Financial discipline is all about making intentional

choices with your money. It means budgeting, saving, and investing wisely. It's about managing your expenses so that you can build wealth over time."

Key Principles of Financial Discipline:

Create a Budget

Mr. Sharma explains: "A budget helps you track where your money is going and ensures that you're not spending more than you earn. It gives you control over your financial life."

Example:

Rajan begins tracking his expenses. He realizes he's spending a significant amount on dining out, and with a few simple changes, he can save more each month.

Pay Yourself First

Mr. Sharma: "This is a simple rule: pay yourself first before spending on anything else. That means saving and investing a portion of your income as soon as you get paid."

Example:

Rajan starts setting aside 20% of his monthly salary into a savings account and investment fund, making sure it's prioritized before paying bills or buying discretionary items.

Cut Unnecessary Expenses

Mr. Sharma: "Look at where your money is going. Eliminate expenses that don't add value to your life."

Example:

Rajan decides to cancel a gym membership he rarely uses and switches to a more affordable home workout routine. This decision saves him ☐ 1,500 per month, which he reallocates to investments.

Avoid Debt Traps

Mr. Sharma: "Avoid high-interest debts, especially credit card debt. Debt can quickly spiral out of control and hinder your ability to save and invest."

Example:

Rajan has credit card debt, and he decides to pay it off by diverting the money he would have spent on unnecessary purchases toward clearing the balance.

Set Clear Financial Goals

Mr. Sharma: "Setting goals helps you stay focused and gives you something to work towards. Whether it's saving for a house, your child's education, or retirement, clear goals give you direction."

Example:

Rajan sets a goal to save ☐ 5,00,000 for his child's education in the next 10 years. This goal motivates him to increase his monthly savings and adjust his lifestyle.

The Magic of Consistency:

Mr. Sharma: "Consistency is the backbone of financial discipline. It's not about making huge changes overnight, but about making small, consistent decisions that add up over time."

Real-Life Example:

Ravi's Consistent Investment:

Ravi started investing ☐ 5,000 per month in an SIP (Systematic Investment Plan) in an equity mutual fund at the age of 25. By the time he turned 40, he had accumulated ☐ 20 lakh, all thanks to consistent, small investments.

Ravi's Lesson: "It wasn't about big chunks of money. It was about doing the same thing every month without fail."

The Role of Patience in Wealth Building:

Rajan: "But, Dad, I want quick results! How long will it take for me to see real wealth?"

Mr. Sharma: "Ah, that's the biggest misconception. Patience is key. It's not about instant gratification; it's about letting your money grow over time."

Example:

Asha's Long-Term Investment:

Asha invested ☐ 10,000 every month in a mutual fund for 15 years. After 15 years, her investment had grown to ☐ 25 lakh, thanks to compounding and market growth.

Asha's Lesson: "It was hard at first, but I trusted the process. The longer you stay invested, the greater the power of compounding."

Building a Legacy:

Mr. Sharma: "Financial discipline isn't just about you. It's about leaving a legacy for your children, your grandchildren, and the generations to come."

Example:

The Sharma Family Legacy:

Mr. Sharma invested wisely throughout his life, ensuring that his wealth continued to grow. He passed on the importance of saving, investing, and living within means to Rajan.

Rajan is now teaching his children the same values, ensuring that the financial lessons he learned will live on for generations.

Tools to Help You Stay Disciplined:

Priya, who joins the conversation: "There are a lot of tools that can help you stay disciplined with your finances. Let me share a few."

Budgeting Apps

Apps like **Mint, YNAB (You Need a Budget)**, and **Wally** help you track your spending, set savings goals, and categorize your expenses automatically.

Automated Transfers

Setting up **automatic transfers** to your savings and investment accounts ensures that you pay yourself first without forgetting or delaying.

Financial Calendars and Reminders

Tools like **Google Calendar** or **Trello** can help you track your financial goals, important payments, and investment reviews.

The Power of Education:

Mr. Sharma: "One of the most powerful tools for financial discipline is continuous learning. The more you know, the better your decisions will be."

Example:

Nina's Financial Knowledge:

Nina took a personal finance course and learned about tax planning, investment strategies, and debt management. This knowledge helped her make smarter financial decisions, and she became debt-free in 3 years.

The Road to Financial Freedom:

Mr. Sharma: "Remember, Rajan, financial freedom is not about how much you make, but about how much you keep. It's about making conscious choices, living below your means, and investing for the future. With financial discipline, you can build a lasting legacy for your family and secure your future."

Key Takeaways:

1. **Budgeting and Tracking Expenses:**
   A budget gives you control over your money and helps you prioritize saving and investing.
2. **Pay Yourself First:**
   Always prioritize savings and investments before spending on discretionary items.
3. **Cutting Unnecessary Expenses:**
   Eliminate wasteful spending and reallocate funds toward investments.
4. **Consistency is Key:**
   Small, consistent actions over time lead to significant wealth accumulation.
5. **Patience Pays Off:**
   Be patient with your investments and allow time for them to grow.

Reflection Question:

"How can you begin implementing financial discipline in your life today?"

Next Chapter Preview:

Chapter 19: The Power of Passive Income — Making Your Money Work for You
Discover how passive income streams can give you financial freedom, allowing your money to work for you even when you sleep.

Chapter 19: "The Power of Passive Income"

Making Your Money Work for You

Rajan's Struggle with Active Income:

Rajan, sitting in his office, looks stressed as he glances at his paycheck.
Rajan (thinking): "It feels like I'm working harder each year, but I'm still stuck in the same place. My salary just doesn't stretch far enough to meet all my goals."

Enter Mr. Sharma.
Mr. Sharma: "Rajan, I can see the weight on your shoulders. Have you ever thought about building passive income streams?"

Rajan: "Passive income? What's that? I'm always working for every rupee I earn. How could money work for me?"

The Concept of Passive Income:

Mr. Sharma smiles knowingly.
Mr. Sharma: "Let me explain. Passive income is money that comes in with minimal effort or time after the initial work or investment. It's not about trading hours for money but about creating systems or investments that generate income even when you're not actively working."

Understanding Active vs. Passive Income:

Mr. Sharma continues, explaining the difference between active and passive income.

Active Income:

This is earned by working, whether as an employee or freelancer. It's the paycheck you get for your time, effort, and skills.

Example:

Rajan's monthly salary is an example of active income. He works 40+ hours a week, and in exchange, he receives his paycheck.

Passive Income:

This is money that comes to you regularly with little ongoing effort. It may require an initial investment of time, effort, or money, but after that, it continues to generate income with little to no active involvement.

Example:

Mr. Sharma shares his own experience of receiving rental income from a property he invested in years ago. Once the property was rented out, the rental income came in regularly without him needing to do much.

Real-Life Examples of Passive Income Streams:

Mr. Sharma:
"Let's look at some examples of passive income streams that can help you build wealth over time."

Real Estate Investment

Mr. Sharma: "Real estate can be an excellent source of passive income. Once you buy a property and rent it out, you can earn monthly rent with little effort."

Example:

Mr. Sharma bought a flat 10 years ago for ₹ 30 lakh, and today, it generates ₹ 20,000 in monthly rent. This income continues to come in every month, regardless of how much effort he puts into it.

Dividend Stocks

Mr. Sharma: "Investing in stocks that pay dividends is another way to generate passive income. You invest your money, and the company shares a portion of its profits with you."

Example:

Rajan decides to invest in **HDFC Bank** and **Reliance Industries**, two companies known for regular dividend payments. Over time, Rajan's investment generates an extra ₹ 2,000 per month in dividends, without him lifting a finger.

Peer-to-Peer Lending (P2P)

Mr. Sharma: "In P2P lending, you lend money to individuals or businesses through platforms like **Lendbox** or **Faircent** and earn interest on your investment."

Example:

Rajan uses a small portion of his savings, ₹ 50,000, to lend money through a P2P platform and starts earning ₹ 4,000 annually in interest, with minimal effort on his part.

Creating Digital Products

Mr. Sharma: "You can also earn passive income by creating digital products, such as e-books, online courses, or software tools, and selling them online."

Example:

Rajan decides to write a financial e-book. After putting in time and effort to write and publish it, the e-book begins generating passive income as people continue to buy it online.

The Power of Compounding in Passive Income:

Rajan: "But does this really work? I mean, will my efforts really pay off?"
Mr. Sharma: "Ah, here's where the magic happens – compounding. Once you start generating passive income, you can reinvest it to create even more income. The longer you let it compound, the bigger the impact."

Example:

Asha's Compounding Journey:

Asha invested ₹ 10,000 in an SIP in mutual funds. Over 10 years, her investment grew thanks to compounding. In the 11th year, she reinvested the returns, and by the 15th year, she had accumulated ₹ 40 lakh. Her initial investment of ₹ 10,000 per month had grown exponentially.

Building a Diversified Passive Income Portfolio:

Mr. Sharma: "The key to building long-term wealth through passive income is diversification. You shouldn't put all your eggs in one basket. Spread your investments across multiple passive income sources to minimize risk and maximize returns."

Example:

Rajan's Diversification Strategy:

Rajan decides to diversify his passive income streams by investing in a combination of real estate (renting out a small apartment), dividend-paying stocks, and a P2P lending platform. By spreading his investments, he reduces the risk of depending on just one income source.

The Importance of Initial Effort:

Rajan: "This sounds great, but doesn't it require a lot of initial work or investment?"
Mr. Sharma: "Yes, there is initial work or capital required, but once that's done, the income keeps coming in passively. It's like planting a tree – it takes time and effort to grow, but once it's established, it provides shade for years."

Example:

Nina's Investment in Real Estate:

Nina saved for years and bought a second-hand property for ☐ 50 lakh. While it took time and effort to find the right property, today, she earns ☐ 35,000 in rent every month. The property has appreciated in value, and her investment continues to grow, both in terms of rental income and capital appreciation.

Overcoming Challenges in Building Passive Income:

Rajan: "But what if I don't have enough capital to invest in real estate or stocks?"
Mr. Sharma: "That's the beauty of passive income – it can start small. You don't need a fortune to begin. You can start by investing small amounts in dividend-paying stocks, mutual funds, or P2P lending."

Example:

Amit's Small Start:

Amit started by investing ₹ 2,000 every month in a mutual fund SIP. Over 5 years, his investment grew, and his returns were reinvested. Though small at first, the income slowly turned into a substantial passive source.

Building Wealth with Patience and Persistence:

Mr. Sharma: "Rajan, remember that building passive income is a long-term strategy. It won't make you rich overnight, but with patience, it can create wealth over time."

Example:

Vikram's Journey:

Vikram invested ₹ 20,000 per month in a combination of stocks, bonds, and real estate for 15 years. By the end of the 15 years, his portfolio was worth ₹ 1 crore, providing him with enough passive income to support his lifestyle.

The Road to Financial Freedom:

Mr. Sharma: "The best part about passive income is that it allows you to achieve financial freedom. You no longer have to depend on a paycheck to survive. Your money works for you, and you can focus on things that matter more in life – family, health, hobbies, and personal growth."

Rajan: "I see now. It's not about earning more, but about making my money work for me."

Key Takeaways:

1. **Understand the Power of Passive Income:**
   Passive income allows you to generate money with little ongoing effort, giving you more freedom.
2. **Diversify Your Passive Income Streams:**
   Don't rely on just one source of passive income. Spread your investments across different platforms.
3. **Start Small and Stay Consistent:**
   Begin with small investments, and stay committed. Over time, your income will grow.
4. **Reinvest Earnings:**
   Let your passive income compound by reinvesting the money you earn.
5. **Be Patient:**
   Building a passive income portfolio takes time, but persistence leads to financial freedom.

Reflection Question:

"What passive income stream can you start today, with the resources you currently have?"

Next Chapter Preview:

Chapter 20: Inflation-Proofing Your Wealth — Building Resilience for the Future
Learn how to protect your hard-earned money from inflation's eroding effects and safeguard your wealth for future generations.

Chapter 20: "Inflation-Proofing Your Wealth"

Building Resilience for the Future

Rajan's Wake-Up Call:

Rajan stares at his investment portfolio, shaking his head in frustration.
Rajan (thinking): "I've been saving and investing for years, but inflation keeps eating away at my returns. I can barely keep up."

Enter Mr. Sharma.
Mr. Sharma: "I can see the concern on your face, Rajan. Inflation is a silent killer when it comes to savings and investments. But don't worry — there are ways to inflation-proof your wealth."

Understanding Inflation and Its Impact:

Mr. Sharma explains inflation in simple terms.
Mr. Sharma: "Inflation is the rise in the cost of goods and services over time, which reduces the purchasing power of money. For example, if inflation is 6%, then what ☐ 100 can buy today will cost ☐ 106 next year. This means your savings and investments need to grow faster than inflation to preserve their value."

The Real Impact of Inflation on Savings:

Mr. Sharma: "Think of it this way: if you keep ☐ 1 lakh in a savings account that gives you a 4% interest rate, and inflation is 6%, you're actually losing money. The interest you earn isn't enough to offset the rising prices of goods and services."

Example:

Rajan's Bank Account:

Rajan has ₹5 lakh in a savings account earning 4% interest. But inflation is at 6%. After one year, his money grows to ₹5.2 lakh, but the real value of that money, after accounting for inflation, is only ₹4.9 lakh in today's terms.

How Inflation Erodes Your Purchasing Power:

Mr. Sharma continues, providing an example to show inflation's real effect.
Mr. Sharma: "Imagine you've saved ₹10 lakh for a big purchase, like a car. But by the time you're ready to buy it, inflation has pushed the car price up by 8%. What you thought would be enough now falls short."

Example:

Rajan's Car Purchase:

Rajan planned to buy a car for ₹8 lakh. However, due to inflation, the car price increased by ₹64,000. By the time he saved the money, his savings were no longer enough. This is the power of inflation working against your goals.

Protecting Your Savings from Inflation:

Mr. Sharma: "So, how do you protect your wealth from inflation? It's not about avoiding inflation but about beating it. You need to invest in assets that have the potential to outpace inflation."

Inflation-Proof Investments:

Mr. Sharma explains various investment tools that can help safeguard against inflation.

Equities (Stocks and Mutual Funds):

Mr. Sharma: "Historically, equities have outperformed inflation. Over the long term, stocks have consistently delivered returns that beat inflation."

Example:

Nina's Investment in Stocks:

Nina invested ₹1 lakh in **Bajaj Finance** five years ago. Over time, the stock price increased by 15% per year on average, far outpacing the 6% inflation rate.

Real Estate:

Mr. Sharma: "Real estate is another strong hedge against inflation. As inflation rises, property values tend to increase as well."

Example:

Vikram's Investment in Property:

Vikram bought a commercial property for ₹40 lakh. Over 10 years, the property value increased by 70%, comfortably outpacing the rate of inflation.

Precious Metals (Gold, Silver):

Mr. Sharma: "Gold is often seen as a safe haven during inflationary times. Its value tends to increase when the purchasing power of currency decreases."

Example:

Amit's Gold Investment:

Amit bought gold coins worth ₹ 2 lakh 5 years ago. Today, the price of gold has risen by 25%, giving him a substantial gain even as inflation erodes the value of money.

Inflation-Linked Bonds (ILBs):

Mr. Sharma: "These are government bonds designed to provide returns that are adjusted for inflation. They are a direct way to protect your investments from inflation."

Example:

Asha's ILB Investment:

Asha invested ₹ 5 lakh in India's **Inflation-Linked Bonds**, which offered returns tied to the Consumer Price Index (CPI). Over time, her investment grew at a rate higher than inflation.

Diversification — A Safety Net Against Inflation:

Mr. Sharma emphasizes the importance of diversification. Mr. Sharma: "To protect your wealth against inflation, you need to diversify your investments. This means spreading your money across different asset classes, so even if one sector doesn't perform well, others may still do better."

Example:

Rajan's Diversified Portfolio:

Rajan invests in a mix of stocks, real estate, and gold. When inflation rises, the value of his real estate and gold increase, while his stocks provide solid returns, keeping his portfolio protected from inflation.

The Power of Long-Term Investing:

Mr. Sharma: "One of the best ways to combat inflation is by taking a long-term approach to investing. The longer your investments are, the more time they have to grow and compound, beating inflation in the process."

Example:

Asha's SIP Investment:

Asha started an SIP (Systematic Investment Plan) of ₹ 10,000 per month in an equity mutual fund. Over 20 years, despite inflation, her portfolio grows to ₹ 60 lakh. The power of compounding allowed her to stay ahead of inflation.

Rebalancing Your Portfolio to Stay Ahead of Inflation:

Mr. Sharma: "Inflation is dynamic — it changes over time. So, you need to review and adjust your portfolio regularly to make sure it continues to beat inflation. For example, if you notice that certain assets are underperforming, you may need to shift funds to more inflation-resistant investments like stocks or real estate."

Building a Future-Proof Financial Strategy:

Mr. Sharma: "Rajan, by understanding inflation and investing wisely, you can create a financial strategy that keeps your wealth growing, even in an inflationary environment."

Example:

Vikram's Inflation-Proof Strategy:

Vikram continuously adjusts his investment portfolio based on market conditions and inflation forecasts. He stays invested in stocks, real estate, and gold, ensuring that his wealth continues to grow, no matter what inflation does.

Key Takeaways:

1. **Understand Inflation's Impact:**
   Inflation erodes the purchasing power of money, and you need to ensure your savings grow faster than inflation to preserve their value.
2. **Invest in Assets that Outpace Inflation:**
   Stocks, real estate, precious metals, and inflation-linked bonds are strong options for beating inflation.
3. **Diversify Your Portfolio:**
   Spread your investments across different asset classes to protect your wealth from inflation's effects.
4. **Invest for the Long Term:**
   The longer your investments are, the more time they have to grow and beat inflation.
5. **Review and Rebalance Regularly:**
   Inflation is constantly changing, so it's crucial to regularly review and adjust your portfolio to stay ahead of inflation.

Reflection Question:

"How can you adjust your investment strategy today to start beating inflation and growing your wealth?"

Next Chapter Preview:

Chapter 21: The Road to Financial Independence — Creating Your Path to Wealth
Learn how to take control of your financial future, achieve financial independence, and secure a stress-free retirement by building and managing your wealth effectively.

Chapter 21: "The Road to Financial Independence"

Creating Your Path to Wealth

The Dream of Financial Freedom:

Ravi sits in his small apartment, staring at his monthly bills.
Ravi (thinking): "I work hard every day, but I can't seem to save enough. How will I ever be financially free?"

Enter Mr. Sharma.
Mr. Sharma: "Ravi, financial freedom isn't about working harder; it's about working smarter. With the right strategy, you can make your money work for you."

What Does Financial Independence Mean?

Mr. Sharma: "Financial independence means having enough income from your investments, assets, and business ventures to cover your living expenses without needing a regular paycheck."

Ravi (curious): "So, you're saying I don't have to rely on my job forever?"

Mr. Sharma (nodding): "Exactly. Imagine waking up every morning without the pressure of having to work for money. That's the power of financial independence."

The Financial Independence Equation:

Mr. Sharma: "To achieve financial independence, you need to follow three key steps: increase your savings, grow your investments, and generate passive income."

Ravi (confused): "But how do I get there from where I am now?"

Mr. Sharma: "Let me break it down for you. The first step is to increase your savings rate, which is the percentage of your income you save and invest."

Step 1 — Increase Your Savings Rate:

Mr. Sharma explains how increasing your savings rate can accelerate the journey to financial independence.
Mr. Sharma: "The more you save, the more money you have to invest. A simple way to do this is by cutting down on unnecessary expenses."

Example:

Ravi's Monthly Budget:

Ravi earns ₹60,000 per month, but his monthly expenses are ₹55,000. By cutting back on dining out, subscriptions, and impulse purchases, he manages to save ₹10,000 every month. Over a year, that's ₹1.2 lakh, which can be invested.

Mr. Sharma: "If you want to speed up the process, consider increasing your savings rate to 20-30% of your income. The more you save, the faster your money works for you."

Step 2 — Grow Your Investments:

Mr. Sharma: "Next, you need to grow your money by investing in assets that appreciate over time. Your savings alone won't be enough to beat inflation and build wealth — you need your money to grow."

Mr. Sharma: "Stocks, mutual funds, real estate, and even starting a business are some of the best ways to grow your wealth. Let me give you some examples."

Stock Market Investments:

Mr. Sharma: "If you invested ₹1 lakh in the Nifty 50 index five years ago, your money would have grown by around 10% annually. That's a solid return that beats inflation and allows your money to grow."

Example:

Ravi's Investment in Mutual Funds:

Ravi invested ₹10,000 per month in an equity mutual fund SIP. Over five years, his investment grew to ₹8 lakh, thanks to the power of compounding. This amount is now working for him, earning returns that outpace inflation.

Real Estate:

Mr. Sharma: "Investing in property is another way to grow your wealth. As inflation rises, the value of real estate typically appreciates, which helps you keep up with inflation and build long-term wealth."

Example:

Amit's Property Investment:

Amit bought a small apartment for ₹40 lakh. Over ten years, the property increased in value by 60%. Today, the property is worth ₹64 lakh, providing him with a nice capital gain, alongside rental income.

Step 3 — Generating Passive Income:

Mr. Sharma: "Passive income is income that comes in regularly without you having to actively work for it. This is the key to achieving financial independence."

Example:

Ravi's Rental Income:

Ravi bought a small flat with a loan for ☐ 50 lakh and started renting it out for ☐ 25,000 per month. After paying off the loan EMI, Ravi earns ☐ 15,000 every month in passive income. This is money that comes in every month, even while he sleeps.

Mr. Sharma: "Other examples of passive income include dividend income from stocks, interest from bonds, and income from a business that doesn't require your constant involvement."

Building Your Financial Freedom Plan:

Mr. Sharma: "To achieve financial independence, you need to create a roadmap. The best way is by setting clear financial goals."

Step 1: Calculate your current expenses

Understand how much you spend every month and determine how much passive income you need to cover those expenses.

Step 2: Set a target savings rate

Set a realistic target for how much of your income you want to save and invest each month. Start with 10-20%, and increase it over time.

Step 3: Invest in growth assets

Choose a combination of stocks, real estate, and mutual funds to grow your wealth over time.

Step 4: Create multiple passive income streams

Focus on building multiple streams of passive income to achieve true financial independence. This could be through real estate, stocks, or even creating an online business.

The Power of Compound Interest:

Mr. Sharma: "Let me tell you about the magic of compound interest. The earlier you start investing, the more time your money has to grow. Compounding works best over long periods."

Example:

Ravi's SIP Growth:

Ravi starts investing ₹ 5,000 every month in a mutual fund SIP. At an average annual return of 12%, his investment grows to ₹ 9 lakh after 10 years. The power of compounding allows his initial ₹ 5,000 monthly contribution to grow exponentially.

The Importance of Financial Discipline:

Mr. Sharma: "Achieving financial independence doesn't happen overnight. It takes time, patience, and discipline. The key is consistency."

Example:

Nina's Financial Discipline:

Nina started saving ₹ 15,000 per month when she was 25. By the time she turned 40, she had accumulated ₹ 60 lakh through disciplined saving and investing. Her disciplined approach allowed her to live a financially independent life.

The Road Ahead:

Mr. Sharma: "Ravi, achieving financial independence is a journey. It requires planning, action, and discipline, but the rewards are worth it. You can wake up every day knowing that your money is working for you, not the other way around."

Key Takeaways:

1. **Increase Your Savings Rate:**
   Save and invest a significant portion of your income to speed up the journey to financial freedom.
2. **Invest in Growth Assets:**
   Stocks, real estate, and mutual funds are excellent ways to grow your wealth and outpace inflation.
3. **Generate Passive Income:**
   Create passive income streams through investments like real estate or dividend-paying stocks to cover your living expenses.
4. **Set Clear Financial Goals:**
   Create a roadmap with clear goals for saving, investing, and building passive income.
5. **Harness the Power of Compounding:**
   Start early and let compound interest work its magic on your wealth.
6. **Be Consistent:**
   Discipline and consistency are key to achieving financial independence over time.

Reflection Question:

"What steps will you take today to start your journey towards financial independence?"

Next Chapter Preview:

Chapter 22: Navigating Market Volatility — Strategies for Protecting Your Wealth During Uncertainty
Learn how to manage your investments through market ups and downs, using strategic approaches that help you stay on track toward your financial goals.

Chapter 22: "Navigating Market Volatility"

Strategies for Protecting Your Wealth during Uncertainty

The Stormy Market:

Ravi sits in his living room, anxiously watching the financial news.
News Anchor: "Stock markets have plunged by 20% in the last two months, and analysts predict more volatility ahead."

Ravi (worried): "I've invested so much money, and now it's all falling. What if I lose everything?"

Enter Mr. Sharma.
Mr. Sharma (calmly): "Ravi, it's natural to feel anxious during market downturns. But the key to protecting your wealth during these times is to have a strategy."

Understanding Market Volatility:

Mr. Sharma: "Market volatility is a natural part of investing. It happens when the prices of stocks, bonds, or other assets fluctuate significantly in a short period. This could be due to economic changes, political instability, or even global events."

Ravi (nodding): "I understand, but what can I do about it?"

Mr. Sharma: "The first thing you need to do is stay calm and stick to your plan. Panicking and selling off your investments during a downturn can lock in losses. Instead, you should focus on strategies that protect your investments and allow them to weather the storm."

The Importance of Diversification:

Mr. Sharma: "Diversification is your first line of defense against market volatility. It means spreading your investments across different types of assets, sectors, and geographies. The more diversified your portfolio, the less risk you take by relying on any single investment."

Example:

Ravi's Diversified Portfolio:

Ravi has a portfolio with investments in:

Equities (40%): Stocks in various sectors, including technology, finance, and healthcare.

Bonds (30%): Government and corporate bonds for stability and income.

Real Estate (20%): Rental properties that provide regular income and appreciation.

Gold (10%): Gold as a hedge against inflation and currency fluctuations.

Mr. Sharma: "By diversifying, you reduce the impact of a downturn in one sector or asset class. If one investment falls, others may remain stable or even rise."

The Power of Asset Allocation:

Mr. Sharma: "Asset allocation is another key strategy. This involves dividing your investments among different asset classes based on your risk tolerance and investment goals."

Ravi (curious): "But how do I decide how much to allocate to each asset class?"

Mr. Sharma: "A good rule of thumb is to consider your age, time horizon, and risk tolerance. If you're young and have a long time to invest, you can afford to take more risks with stocks. But if you're nearing retirement, you might want to shift more into bonds or other low-risk investments."

Hedging Against Inflation:

Mr. Sharma: "When inflation rises, the real value of your money decreases. This erodes your purchasing power and can lead to lower returns on fixed-income investments. To protect yourself, you need to hedge against inflation."

Ravi: "How do I do that?"

Mr. Sharma: "One way is by investing in assets that tend to rise with inflation, such as stocks, real estate, and commodities like gold."

Example:

Stocks:

Nina's Investment in Stocks:

Nina invested in large-cap stocks, which historically outpace inflation over time. While the market fluctuates, her portfolio grows faster than inflation.

Real Estate:

Amit's Property Investment:

Amit owns rental properties that generate passive income and appreciate over time. As inflation rises, rent prices also tend to increase, providing him with an inflation-proof income stream.

Commodities (like Gold):

Ravi's Gold Investment:

Ravi invested in gold when inflation was rising. Gold is considered a safe haven during periods of high inflation because it tends to hold its value.

Stay Invested — The Importance of Long-Term Thinking:

Mr. Sharma: "When markets are volatile, it's tempting to sell everything and sit out the storm. But that's the worst thing you can do. Remember, markets are cyclical. They go up and down, but historically, they always recover in the long run."

Example:

Ravi's Experience with Market Volatility:

Ravi recalls the 2008 financial crisis when the stock market fell sharply. Many investors panicked and sold off their holdings. However, Ravi held onto his investments and, over the next few years, saw them recover and grow even more than before.

Mr. Sharma: "Staying invested through the ups and downs of the market is critical. The power of compounding can only work if you give it time."

Dollar-Cost Averaging (DCA):

Mr. Sharma: "Dollar-cost averaging (DCA) is a strategy that involves investing a fixed amount of money at regular intervals, regardless of the market's performance. This helps smooth out the effects of market volatility and reduces the risk of making poor investment decisions during market peaks."

Example:

Ravi's SIP Investment:

Ravi invests ₹ 5,000 every month in an equity mutual fund, regardless of whether the market is up or down. Some months, his ₹ 5,000 buys fewer units when prices are high, and other months it buys more when prices are low. Over time, this strategy lowers his average cost per unit, helping him ride out volatility.

Rebalancing Your Portfolio:

Mr. Sharma: "Over time, your asset allocation can drift as certain investments perform better than others. This is why it's important to periodically rebalance your portfolio — to ensure it stays in line with your original investment goals and risk tolerance."

Ravi (questioning): "How often should I rebalance?"

Mr. Sharma: "Rebalance your portfolio at least once a year, or if there's a significant change in your financial situation. This ensures that you're not overexposed to risk, and your portfolio continues to meet your financial goals."

Preparing for Market Downturns:

Mr. Sharma: "No one can predict market downturns, but you can prepare for them. Here are some tips to help you navigate market volatility."

Build an Emergency Fund:

Ensure you have 3-6 months' worth of living expenses set aside in a liquid, low-risk savings account.

Focus on Cash Flow:

Generate passive income streams through real estate, dividend stocks, or other investments that provide regular income.

Stay Calm and Avoid Panic Selling:

Market downturns are temporary. Stay invested for the long term and avoid making emotional decisions during times of volatility.

The Road Ahead:

Mr. Sharma: "Ravi, market volatility is inevitable, but it doesn't have to derail your financial journey. By diversifying your investments, protecting yourself from inflation, and staying calm during tough times, you can weather any storm."

Ravi (smiling): "Thanks, Mr. Sharma. I feel more confident now. I'm going to stick to my plan, stay invested, and let my wealth grow, no matter what happens in the markets."

Key Takeaways:

1. **Diversify Your Investments:**
   Spread your money across different asset classes to reduce risk and protect against market downturns.
2. **Asset Allocation is Key:**
   Adjust your investments based on your risk tolerance and time horizon.
3. **Hedge Against Inflation:**
   Invest in stocks, real estate, and commodities like gold to protect your wealth from inflation.
4. **Stay Invested for the Long Term:**
   Don't panic during market downturns. Stick to your investment strategy and trust that the market will recover.
5. **Dollar-Cost Averaging:**
   Invest regularly, regardless of market conditions, to smooth out market volatility and reduce the risk of making poor investment decisions.

6. **Rebalance Your Portfolio:**
   Regularly review and adjust your investments to ensure they remain aligned with your financial goals.
7. **Prepare for Market Downturns:**
   Build an emergency fund, focus on cash flow, and avoid emotional decision-making during volatile times.

Reflection Question:

"What strategies will you adopt to protect your wealth during periods of market volatility?"

Next Chapter Preview:

Chapter 23: The Role of Financial Literacy in Protecting Your Wealth
Discover how financial education empowers you to make informed decisions, avoid common mistakes, and navigate the complex world of investments.

Chapter 23: "The Role of Financial Literacy"

Protecting Your Wealth

The Seed of Knowledge:

Ravi is sitting at his desk, staring at a mountain of financial papers. His investments are scattered across multiple accounts, and he feels overwhelmed.
Ravi (frustrated): "I just don't understand this! Why do some investments work for me, and others don't? It feels like I'm guessing with my money."

Enter Mr. Sharma, as always calm and composed.
Mr. Sharma: "Ravi, the problem isn't that you don't have the right investments. It's that you haven't taken the time to understand the financial tools at your disposal. Without financial literacy, it's easy to fall into traps, even when you have good intentions."

Ravi (confused): "So, you're saying I need to learn more about this?"

Mr. Sharma (nodding): "Exactly. Financial literacy is the foundation of making informed, intelligent decisions about your money. It empowers you to protect your wealth and grow it effectively, even in the face of inflation and market volatility."

What is Financial Literacy?

Mr. Sharma (explaining): "At its core, financial literacy is the ability to understand and use various financial skills effectively. This includes budgeting, saving, investing, managing debt, understanding inflation, and making decisions about risk and reward. It's about understanding how money works in the world and in your life."

Ravi (thoughtful): "That makes sense, but where do I start?"

Mr. Sharma: "The journey to financial literacy begins with education. You don't need a finance degree to understand the basics. Just take it one step at a time."

The Importance of Understanding Money:

Mr. Sharma (walking towards a whiteboard): "Let's break it down. Understanding money isn't just about how much you earn—it's about how you manage and grow that money. Here are a few key concepts you need to understand to start building financial literacy."

Income vs. Expenses:
"The first step is knowing the difference between your income (the money you earn) and your expenses (the money you spend). The goal is to spend less than you earn and save the difference."

Example:

Ravi's Budget Breakdown:

Ravi earns ☐ 60,000 per month, and his expenses total ☐ 50,000. This leaves him with ☐ 10,000 to save or invest each month. However, he doesn't know where to allocate this money yet. Financial literacy would help him make better choices.

The Power of Saving:
"Next, learn the importance of saving. Building an emergency fund—typically 3-6 months of living expenses—is crucial. Beyond that, saving for short-term goals, like buying a car, or long-term goals, like retirement, requires discipline."

Example:

Amit's Emergency Fund:

Amit decided to start an emergency fund and managed to save ₹ 50,000 in six months. When he lost his job due to the pandemic, this emergency fund gave him the cushion he needed to survive without going into debt.

The Power of Compound Interest and Time:

Mr. Sharma (writing on the board): "The next important concept is compound interest. This is the idea that the money you invest earns interest, and that interest earns more interest over time."

Ravi (curious): "So, the longer I invest, the more my money grows?"

Mr. Sharma: "Yes, exactly. Let me show you an example."

Example:

Compound Interest Explained:

Ravi invests ₹ 10,000 in a mutual fund earning 8% annual return. After one year, he'll have ₹ 10,800. But in the second year, the interest is calculated on ₹ 10,800, not just the original ₹ 10,000. This leads to exponential growth over time.

Calculation:

Year 1: ₹ 10,000 + (8% of ₹ 10,000) = ₹ 10,800

Year 2: ₹ 10,800 + (8% of ₹ 10,800) = ₹ 11,664

By the 10th year, his ₹ 10,000 has grown to ₹ 21,589!

Mr. Sharma: "This is why it's crucial to start investing early. The more time your money has to compound, the greater your wealth will grow."

Managing Debt Wisely:

Mr. Sharma (turning serious): "Now, Ravi, let's talk about debt. Debt can be a powerful tool if used wisely, but if mismanaged, it can also become a burden."

Ravi (nodding): "I've heard that before, but how do I know when debt is a problem?"

Mr. Sharma: "It becomes a problem when the interest you pay on your debt is higher than the return you're earning on your investments. For example, credit card debt often comes with interest rates of 15-20%, which is higher than most investments can earn."

Example:

Ravi's Credit Card Debt:

Ravi has ☐ 50,000 in credit card debt with an interest rate of 18% per year. He only pays the minimum due each month, but the debt keeps growing. Meanwhile, he has ☐ 30,000 invested in a stock fund earning an average of 10% annually. Ravi's money in the stock fund is growing, but his credit card debt is growing faster, effectively eroding his wealth.

Mr. Sharma: "The solution? Pay off high-interest debt first, before focusing on investing. The quicker you eliminate debt, the faster you can grow your wealth."

Investment Tools and Strategies:

Mr. Sharma: "Ravi, let's talk about investments. With financial literacy, you'll understand the different investment tools available and how to choose the right ones for your goals."

Stocks and Equity Mutual Funds:
"Stocks give you ownership in companies, and equity mutual funds

pool money from multiple investors to buy a diversified set of stocks. While they offer high potential returns, they also come with higher risk."

Bonds and Fixed Income Securities:
"Bonds are loans to governments or corporations that pay interest. They offer more stability than stocks but generally provide lower returns."

Real Estate:
"Investing in property can provide steady income through rentals and appreciation over time. It's an excellent hedge against inflation but requires a larger upfront investment."

Gold and Commodities:
"Gold and other commodities, like silver or oil, can act as a hedge against inflation and are tangible assets that tend to maintain their value over time."

Retirement Accounts (PF, PPF, NPS):
"Retirement-focused accounts like Provident Fund (PF), Public Provident Fund (PPF), and the National Pension Scheme (NPS) offer tax advantages and long-term growth potential."

Practical Steps to Improve Your Financial Literacy:

Mr. Sharma: "Now, Ravi, let's talk about how you can improve your financial literacy and start making smarter decisions."

1. Read Financial Books and Blogs:
"Start with books like *The Intelligent Investor* by Benjamin Graham or blogs like *The Financial Samurai* to get a deeper understanding of investing."

2. Take Online Courses:
"Websites like Coursera, Khan Academy, and Udemy offer courses on personal finance and investing for beginners."

3. Seek Professional Advice:
"If you're unsure about complex financial decisions, don't hesitate to consult with a certified financial advisor."

4. Practice What You Learn:
"Start small. Open a small investment account or a high-yield savings account and experiment with different strategies. The more you practice, the more confident you'll become."

The Road to Financial Freedom:

Mr. Sharma (smiling): "By improving your financial literacy, you're putting yourself in control of your money. No longer will inflation, market volatility, or poor financial decisions keep you from reaching your goals. Instead, you'll make educated choices, protect your wealth, and secure your future."

Ravi (confidently): "Thank you, Mr. Sharma. I'm ready to learn more and take control of my finances. I know it's a journey, but I'm starting now."

Key Takeaways:

1. **Financial Literacy is Essential:**
   Understand the basics of budgeting, saving, investing, and managing debt to make informed decisions with your money.
2. **Compound Interest is Powerful:**
   Start investing early to take full advantage of the exponential growth that compound interest offers.
3. **Manage Debt Wisely:**
   Avoid high-interest debt and focus on paying it off before investing in high-return assets.
4. **Use a Variety of Investment Tools:**
   Diversify your investments across stocks, bonds, real estate, and commodities to balance risk and return.
5. **Continuous Learning:**
   Commit to learning about personal finance through books,

courses, and professional advice to improve your financial decisions.

Reflection Question:

"What are some financial tools you'll explore first to start building your knowledge and improve your financial literacy?"

Pro Tips for Protecting Your Wealth from Inflation and Making Smart Financial Choices

1. Start with a Financial Plan

Before diving into investments or savings, create a solid financial plan. This means setting clear goals—whether it's building an emergency fund, buying a home, or saving for retirement. Your plan should include:

Income and expense tracking: Know exactly where your money is going.

Goal prioritization: Which goals are most important right now (e.g., debt repayment or building savings)?

Timeline: Set a timeline for achieving these goals.

Pro Tip: Use financial apps like Mint or YNAB (You Need a Budget) to automate expense tracking and budgeting. They provide visual reports to help you see where you can improve.

2. Automate Your Savings and Investments

The key to building wealth without overthinking it is automation. Set up automatic transfers from your salary account to savings or investment accounts.

Emergency fund: Aim to save 3-6 months of living expenses.

Retirement savings: Contribute to retirement accounts like PF, PPF, or NPS regularly. Even a small amount compounds over time.

Pro Tip: Try the "50/30/20 Rule" for budgeting:

- 50% of your income to needs (rent, utilities, etc.)
- 30% to wants (eating out, entertainment)
- 20% to savings and investments.

3. Understand Inflation's Impact on Your Savings

Inflation erodes the purchasing power of your money. If your savings are sitting in a regular savings account with low-interest rates, they may not even keep up with inflation.

Invest in assets that can beat inflation, like stocks, real estate, or inflation-linked bonds.

Consider government bonds or Treasury Inflation-Protected Securities (TIPS) that are designed to adjust with inflation.

Pro Tip: Check inflation rates before making long-term savings decisions. Historically, equities and real estate have provided returns higher than inflation, while savings accounts tend to lag behind.

4. Diversify Your Investment Portfolio

Don't put all your money into one investment. Diversification helps spread risk and protects you from market volatility.

Equities (stocks) offer high growth potential but come with higher risk.

Bonds and fixed income provide stable returns and act as a cushion in volatile markets.

Commodities like gold can hedge against inflation.

Pro Tip: A well-balanced portfolio for a conservative investor might be:

- 40% stocks
- 40% bonds
- 20% real estate or commodities.

For more aggressive growth, the stock percentage can increase, but always align your risk tolerance with your asset allocation.

5. Invest in Learning—Not Just Money

The best investment you can make is in yourself. Financial literacy is the cornerstone of wealth-building. Stay curious and continue learning about personal finance.

Take free courses online (e.g., Coursera, Khan Academy).

Read financial books and blogs to stay updated on investment strategies.

Pro Tip: Read books like *Rich Dad Poor Dad* by Robert Kiyosaki or *The Intelligent Investor* by Benjamin Graham to learn more about money management and investing. These foundational texts can reshape your perspective on wealth.

6. Regularly Review Your Financial Portfolio

A financial plan or investment strategy is not something you set and forget. You need to review it regularly (at least once every 6 months) to ensure it's still in line with your goals.

Are your investments performing as expected?

Are there new investment opportunities (e.g., index funds, real estate)?

Has your life situation changed (e.g., marriage, kids, career change)?

Pro Tip: Use financial tools like **Personal Capital** or **Morningstar** to monitor your portfolio's performance and asset allocation.

7. Focus on Long-Term Wealth, Not Short-Term Gains:

Short-term fluctuations in the stock market or sudden opportunities for quick profit might seem tempting, but the real wealth comes from long-term, steady investing.

Focus on assets with solid long-term growth potential.

Avoid speculative investments or "get-rich-quick" schemes.

Pro Tip: Stick to dollar-cost averaging—invest a fixed amount regularly, regardless of market conditions. This reduces the impact of market volatility and helps avoid trying to time the market.

8. Understand Your Risk Tolerance:

Different financial tools carry different levels of risk. The key is to invest according to your comfort level, particularly when inflation is high.

Conservative risk tolerance: Stick to bonds, fixed deposits, or mutual funds.

Aggressive risk tolerance: Consider stocks, ETFs, or start-ups.

Pro Tip: You can use a **risk tolerance questionnaire** (available online) to better understand your investment style and adjust your portfolio accordingly.

9. Don't Let Emotional Decisions Control Your Money:

Financial markets are volatile, and it's easy to get emotional when things don't go according to plan. Don't make rash decisions during market downturns or when you're feeling uncertain.

Stay calm, review your strategy, and stick to your long-term goals.

Rebalance your portfolio periodically to ensure you are aligned with your goals.

Pro Tip: Use the "Buy and Hold" strategy for long-term investments—once you've made an informed decision, let your investments grow without constant tinkering.

10. Always Have a Safety Net: Build an Emergency Fund:

An emergency fund is your safety net during unexpected life events (medical emergencies, job loss, etc.).

Aim to save 3-6 months' worth of expenses in a liquid, easy-to-access account.

Make sure this fund is separate from your investment accounts.

Pro Tip: Keep your emergency fund in a **high-yield savings account** or a **short-term fixed deposit** to earn a little interest while still keeping it accessible in case of an emergency.

Bonus Tip: Master the Art of Tax Planning:

Tax efficiency is a critical part of wealth-building. Learn about the tax benefits of various financial tools and make sure you're taking advantage of them.

Tax-free accounts: Look for tax-saving investments (e.g., PPF, NPS).

Capital gains tax: Understand the tax treatment of long-term vs. short-term gains.

Pro Tip: *Consult with a tax professional or use tax preparation software to maximize your tax savings and avoid any surprises during tax season.*

By applying these pro tips, you can protect your wealth from inflation, make informed financial decisions, and steadily work towards your financial freedom. The key is staying educated, patient, and consistent in your approach to managing money.

"Empower Your Wealth, Protect Your Future: Master the Art of Saving in an Inflation-Driven World."

www.ingramcontent.com/pod-product-compliance
Lightning Source LLC
Chambersburg PA
CBHW071031240526
45469CB00006BD/2167